The Politics
of Deterrence

*American and Soviet Defense
Policies Compared, 1960–1964*

by

Paul Michael Kozar

McFarland & Company, Inc., Publishers
Jefferson, North Carolina, and London

for Joan

Library of Congress Cataloguing-in-Publication Data

Kozar, Paul Michael, 1948–
The politics of deterrence.

Bibliography: p. 153.
Includes index.
1. United States — Military policy.
2. Soviet Union — Military policy.
3. Deterrence (Strategy)
I. Title.
UA23.k775   1987   355′.0335″73   87-42512

ISBN 0-89950-274-1 (acid-free natural paper)

Printed in the United States of America.

McFarland   Box 611   Jefferson NC 28640

Preface

This study was conceived in the belief that history has an important place in contemporary strategic thought. But a historical perspective alone is insufficient to unravel the complexities of the strategic nuclear equation and to fathom the uncertainties of the future. One also needs to discern the motives and perspectives of the opponent. This demands nothing less than a comparative approach to defense analysis that is firmly grounded in Soviet studies.

I owe a particular debt of gratitude to my mentor, Professor Angela E. Stent, and to the other members of my doctoral dissertation committee, Professors Charles F. Elliott and G. Paul Holman, for their wise counsel. I also wish to express my sincere appreciation to the United States Arms Control and Disarmament Agency for awarding me a Hubert H. Humphrey Fellowship as well as to the Lyndon Baines Johnson Foundation for presenting me with a Moody Grant.

I am indebted to Governor W. Averell Harriman for permitting me to review and cite his personal papers in this study, and to his assistant, Pie Friendly, for her generous help. My research led me to the John F. Kennedy Memorial Library in Boston, Massachusetts, and the Lyndon B. Johnson Library in Austin, Texas, and I thank the members of both staffs, particularly Ronald Whealan and David Humphrey, for their kind support.

Throughout, my parents patiently endured my trials and they remain a source of constant encouragement and support. To Laughlin Austin Campbell, a kindred spirit and a scholar, I owe more than a son-in-law could expect to receive. Finally, I must thank my beloved wife and companion, Joan, to whom this book is gratefully and affectionately dedicated.

iii

Table of Contents

Table of Contents

Introduction

> If we only act for ourselves, to neglect the study of history is not
> prudent; if we are entrusted with the care of others it is not just.
>
> *Samuel Johnson*

The study of Soviet military thought languished for years in the West. Few scholars or policymakers paid any mind to the intellectual ferment that seized the Soviet military and political establishment during the 1950s and early 1960s. There were, however, important exceptions: Herbert Dinerstein, Raymond Garthoff, and Thomas Wolfe in the United States, and John Erickson, Malcolm Mackintosh, and Peter Vigor in Great Britain. Each contributed significantly to the field and their writings set a standard for scholarly research that is no less important.

Nevertheless, it is extremely difficult to assess the influence of these writings on the actual formulation of American defense policy. Even the Soviets' own commentaries on nuclear strategy were dismissed at the time by President Kennedy's men. When asked for his comments on Marshal V.D. Sokolovskiy's treatise, *Military Strategy*, Secretary of Defense Robert McNamara quipped that he had a copy in his office. "This is a tremendously long book," the secretary told the members of the House Subcommittee on Defense Appropriations. "It is written as so many Russian books are, with very imprecise language in places, therefore, it is difficult to interpret."[1] By the mid-1970s, however, the study of Soviet defense policy in general, and Soviet disquisitions on military strategy in particular, had become a cottage industry among Western defense intellectuals. The reasons for this phenomenon deserve a closer look.

Mainstream liberal opinion in the United States welcomed the emergence of strategic parity between the superpowers. Writing a year before the SALT I agreements were signed, Roman Kolkowicz argued that "modern defense technology determines to a large extent the kind

1

of strategic doctrines and policies that will be adopted by the super-powers." Technology, in turn, Kolkowicz observed, has a "leveling effect that subsumes various political, ideological and social differences in various political systems." This, he confidently asserted, would have an "educative effect" on the Soviets and lead to the "progressive strategic convergence of the superpowers."[2] Johan Holst also viewed the SALT negotiations as an "educational exercise" that could reduce the propensities of the United States and the Soviet Union to brandish a hostile mirror image of the other.[3]

The SALT negotiations proved to be anything but an educational exercise. The Soviets were intent upon restricting the deployment of the American anti-ballistic missile program. Only when this goal was in sight were they willing to discuss the chief concern of the United States negotiators, Soviet intercontinental missiles. In short, the Soviets conceived the SALT process "as a means of enhancing their strategic power within a legitimate framework of U.S. acceptance, and not as a vehicle for producing lasting arms control as an end in itself."[4]

The asymmetries of the Interim Agreement, combined with the appearance of a fourth generation of Soviet ICBMs and the rapid deployment of modern Soviet ballistic missile submarines, fueled the concerns of political conservatives that the U.S. defenses were stagnating as the Soviets resolutely drove towards strategic superiority. One of their number, the late Senator Henry Jackson, attached an amendment to the Senate's ratification of the Interim Agreement and the ABM Treaty that required future strategic arms limitation agreements to be based on the principle of equal force levels.

The subsequent SALT II negotiations corresponded with an energized Soviet foreign policy and increasing disenchantment in the United States with the value of detente. A variety of views appeared on how to enhance the credibility of U.S. nuclear deterrence and to bolster American foreign policy. At the risk of oversimplification, one could discern two distinct perspectives on the issue. The "minimalist" approach to national defense views nuclear war as *unthinkable* and *unwinnable*. The acquisition of nuclear strength, in excess of the minimum needed to retaliate to a direct attack, diminishes U.S. security and simply fuels the arms race. The "maximalists" consider U.S. strategic superiority to be the only reliable policy choice. They contend that the Soviets do not share the American affinity for equivalent forces and mutual deterrence. Therefore, in the absence of overwhelming nuclear strength, the U.S. is judged by the "maximalists" to be unable to deter the offensive deployment of Soviet military power.

A taste of this dispute was offered by the American Enterprise Institute in a 1972 debate between Senator James L. Buckley of New York and Paul C. Warnke, former Assistant Secretary of Defense for International Security Affairs and Pentagon General Counsel. Buckley argued that Soviet strategists thought in vastly different terms than their American counterparts. Soviet military literature, he said, emphasizes not deterrence but the need to emerge relatively stronger than the United States in the event of a nuclear war. Buckley cited as evidence the Soviet leaders' great effort to "minimize the vulnerability of their civilian population to nuclear attack."[5]

In Warnke's view, "a conflict in which victory is measured in relative megadeaths is a war with no winners." Poverty, crime and a deteriorating physical and social environment "represent a danger to our national security at least equivalent to that which we face from alien and militant ideologies." Warnke contended that the U.S. could afford to "take the initiative in restraint while looking for reciprocal restraint from the Soviet Union." "As a superpower, Russia has only one example to follow. We can be quite sure that it will follow any bad example we provide. We can hope that the process of 'superpower aping' will extend to good examples as well."[6]

One of the most articulate and experienced exponents of the "maximalist" perspective is Paul H. Nitze. In his words, there is no substitute for U.S. "strategic nuclear preponderance" to offset "Soviet military superiority at the periphery and to deter its offensive employment." Without superiority, the U.S. is inhibited from contesting the expansion of Soviet influence abroad.[7] Others, such as Colin Gray and Keith Payne, stress the importance of the positive, as opposed to the deterrent, mission of U.S. strategic nuclear forces to support U.S. foreign policy — for example, the commitment to defend Western Europe. This mission, they contend, requires forces "that would enable a president to initiate strategic nuclear use for coercive, though politically defensive, purposes." In other words, a military strategy designed to defeat the Soviet Union on the nuclear battlefield and destroy its system of political control.[8]

During the course of a 1977 interview, Paul Warnke was asked to respond to indications that the Soviet leadership might believe that a nuclear war was winnable.

> In my view, this kind of thinking is on a level of abstraction which is unrealistic. It seems to be that instead of talking in those terms, which would indulge what I regard as the primitive aspects of Soviet nuclear doctrine, we ought to be trying to educate them into the real

world of strategic nuclear weapons, which is that nobody could possibly win.[9]

His answer drew a vitriolic retort from Richard Pipes. "There is ample evidence," Pipes argued, "that the Soviet military say what they mean, and usually mean what they say." The evidence, drawn from Soviet military writings, suggested to Pipes that "while Soviet military doctrine recognizes the devastation of an all-out nuclear war, its outcome would not be mutual suicide." Rather, "the country better prepared for it and in possession of a superior strategy would win and emerge as a viable society."[10]

The notion that mutual deterrence was really an illusion conjured by Western defense intellectuals found support in an article by John Erickson, entitled, appropriately, "The Chimera of Mutual Deterrence." Erickson argued that "deterrence as a *concept* has never held much appeal for the Soviet military: the terms *ustrashenie* and *zderzhivanie* are rarely used, while *oborona* (defense) increasingly denotes the 'deterrent' concept." In his opinion, deterrence remained a derivative notion to the Soviets. "It is commonly assumed in the West that if war comes, then deterrence has failed." But the Soviets, according to Erickson, consider "deterrence" to be only one element in a defense policy that regards the development of a "war fighting capability" as essential to any form of "deterrence posture."[11]

The Pipes article in *Commentary* provoked a new round in the debate. Raymond Garthoff accused critics like Pipes of being insufficiently aware of the record. In his judgment, the Soviet political leaders believe "that the need to avoid a nuclear war can be served by prudent actions within a framework of mutual strategic deterrence between the Soviet Union and the United States."[12]

Bernard Brodie responded to Pipes' thesis by asking, "Who in the Soviet Union thinks they can fight and win a nuclear war?" Brodie noted that Pipes failed to mention the name of a single Soviet political leader in answer to the question. Moreover, Brodie was convinced that the entire notion was a canard. Should nuclear deterrence fail, the only rational response, he advised, "should surely be to terminate [the exchange] as quickly as possible and with the least amount of damage possible on both sides."[13] Michael Howard concurred with a warning that "to engage in a nuclear war, to attempt to use strategic nuclear weapons for 'warfighting' would be to enter a realm of the unknown and the unknowable, and what little we do know about it is appalling."[14]

The question of whether the Soviet Union accepts the term

"mutual deterrence" is probably of little real analytic value. As Robert Legvold observes, neither the United States nor the Soviet Union believes in distinguishing deterrence from defense. "Every American Secretary of Defense underscores the indissoluable link between reliable deterrence and the ability to defend, meaning the ability to fight wars; and Soviet speakers have often enough denied both the utility and the feasibility of defending for anything other than the deterrence of war." According to Legvold, the crucial difference in approach is a consequence of how each has conceptualized nuclear deterrence. The American theory of deterrence is really a theory of bargaining extrapolated from the economic principle of maximizing benefits while minimizing losses. In contrast, the Soviets seek to perfect a theory of war in which deterrence is a residual benefit. "As a result, where the American strategic deterrent is made to cope with a broad range of threats beyond that of nuclear attack, the Soviet Union tends to expect her strategic nuclear forces only to deter others' resort to (strategic) nuclear war."[15]

One of the important benefits of this debate has been to create a greater awareness of the need to develop the intellectual discipline of comparative military doctrine.[16] A monograph by Ken Booth entitled *Strategy and Ethnocentrism* represents an important and novel contribution to this endeavor. Booth attributes the frequent failure of military strategy to adequately discern an opponent's intentions to the ethnocentricity of its practitioners. His suggested improvements include a greater appreciation of strategic history and a greater awareness of the value of Russian area studies to the field of strategic studies.[17]

The purpose of this study is to provide a historical setting for contemporary strategic discourse. The basic assumptions of current American and Soviet nuclear strategy were formulated during the early 1960s. The American strategies of assured destruction and damage limitation received their most complete expression during this period. The Soviets themselves were engaged in a comparable review of military doctrine at the same time. The emergence of the Strategic Rocket Forces at the pinnacle of the Soviet military hierarchy in January 1960 appeared to signal a significant shift in Soviet thinking away from its traditional reliance on massive land armies. By 1964, however, the Soviets were moving towards a combined arms theory of warfare and laying the basis for the qualitative and quantitative expansion of their intercontinental nuclear forces on land and at sea.

My approach to comparative defense policy emphasizes the relationship between military strategy and the foreign policy milieu. The structure of the study illuminates this analytic approach. The first requirement was to determine how President John F. Kennedy and Premier Nikita S. Khrushchev approached the issue of nuclear deterrence and to examine the interaction between Soviet and American foreign policy at this juncture of the Cold War. Chapter 1 chronicles the divergence in security interests between the United States and the Soviet Union prior to the Cuban missile crisis. Chapter 2 presents the key trends in postwar Soviet and American military thought and looks closely at how the military requirements for nuclear deterrence were defined by Secretary of Defense Robert S. McNamara and his opposite number in the Soviet Union, Marshal Rodion Ya. Malinovskiy.

The political and military dimensions of nuclear deterrence converge in Chapter 3's discussion of force posture and the Kennedy Administration's attempts to secure Soviet adherence to an American definition of strategic stability. Although the superpowers remain the preeminent actors on the world stage, the character of the strategic equation has been influenced as much by the ambitions of their allies as by the political competition between the United States and the Soviet Union. Chapter 4 looks at the effect of national nuclear deterrents on alliance politics during the early 1960s, and how the threat of proliferation contributed to a convergence in U.S. and Soviet security interests. The Cuban missile crisis proved to be the impetus for this collaboration as well as a test of nuclear deterrence itself. Chapter 5 presents a case study of the crisis and pays particular attention to its origin and its aftermath. The conclusions of the study are outlined in Chapter 6.

Any comparative study involving the Soviet Union is bound to be subject to a degree of distortion by the very secrecy of the Soviet political system. This, of course, is especially true in matters of defense and foreign affairs. Rarely, if ever, does the researcher garner more than a glimpse of the actual bargaining involved in the formulation of Soviet national security policy. The principal actors are identifiable, and one can even infer their policy perspectives on the basis of institutional affiliation. But the Kremlin's political aviary of hawks and doves is rarely obvious.

American archives obviously provide a more diverse body of source material. Admittedly, this has caused a relative imbalance with Soviet sources. The compensatory factor, however, proved to be Nikita Khrushchev himself. Doubts may linger about the authenticity of Khrushchev's multi-volume memoir, but the ideas expressed by Khrushchev in retirement are remarkably consistent with the utterances of Khrushchev the politician.

Chapter 1

Kennedy, Khrushchev and the Cold War

> Very near the heart of all foreign affairs is the relationship between policy and military power.
>
> McGeorge Bundy

The Cold War was fought in the shadows of back alleys and on Asian battlefields; over the air waves and in print; on the assembly line and in the board room; at the ballot box and in the streets. The battle for the hearts and minds of the uncommitted was dwarfed, however, by the one war neither Washington nor Moscow could afford to win or lose. The conduct of world affairs changed forever after Hiroshima and Nagasaki. An obvious statement no doubt, but one worth repeating. For the first time in history, the diplomatic value of military force was hamstrung by its potential for national suicide.

Before the Cuban missile crisis, both sides refused to recognize their common security interests. The diplomacy of the Cold War was perceived as a zero-sum game in the parlance of today; a political victory by one superpower was tantamount to an irreversible setback for the other. The United States strove to contain the outward thrust of the Soviet Union. Stalin and his successors were equally intent upon breaking the capitalist encirclement of the Eastern bloc. Neither strategy required the opponent's cooperation. Nuclear deterrence simply reinforced two incompatible views of the strategic balance. The Cuban missile crisis changed this calculus. Each side came away from the Caribbean brink with a sober appreciation of the dangers of nuclear war and of their mutual stake in preventing such a catastrophe. The path from mutual hostility to competitive coexistence was blazed by two very different men, one the son of a Boston millionaire, the other the son of a Russian miner.

The Kennedy Perspective

John Kennedy's introduction to Soviet Russia came at an early age. The twenty-one year old Harvard undergraduate traveled to England in February 1939 with a semester's leave in hand and the desire to witness Europe's agony for himself. When young Kennedy arrived in Moscow, he was assisted by Charles Bohlen, then a junior Foreign Service Officer at the American Embassy. Kennedy toured European Russia extensively, frequently shuttling between stops aboard a ramshackle Soviet aircraft. The experience left Kennedy with the memory of a "crude, backward, hopelessly bureaucratic country."[1] Stalin's Russia may have been of no immediate interest to Kennedy, but Bohlen recalled that Kennedy displayed an open-mindedness about the Soviet Union during his short stay in Moscow.[2]

Returning to Cambridge in September, Kennedy began to compose his honors thesis on Britain's reaction to Hitler's aggressive policies in the late 1930s. His thesis attracted a much wider readership in 1940 as a book entitled *Why England Slept*. Kennedy's conclusions revealed a sober appreciation of the totalitarian threat to democracy. Hitler's victory at Munich, he argued, was not simply the fault of a myopic Tory government. The appeasement policies championed by Stanley Baldwin and Neville Chamberlain were symptomatic of the apathy, avarice, and pacifism endemic to capitalist societies. Without strong leadership and a powerful national defense, Kennedy warned, the Western democracies would perish in a war with totalitarianism. "What we need," he concluded, "is an armed guard that will wake up when the fire first starts or, better yet, one that will not permit the fire to start at all."[3]

Twenty years later, John Kennedy stood at the threshold of the American presidency. The night before his first meeting with President Eisenhower on December 6, 1960, Kennedy perused a paper on the *Political Implications of Posture Choices* by Herbert Goldhamer of the Rand Corporation.[4] According to this research memorandum, the new administration stood to profit politically from an expansion of American strategic nuclear capabilities. Goldhamer considered Soviet nuclear blackmail the most serious threat to U.S. national security. The most effective means to counter such dangers was "an *offensive* capability, that is a capability that can ... induce fear in the enemy [and] ... can generate confidence among our allies." Goldhamer warned his readers that the American public would hesitate to support a military buildup without an assurance that "their government is actively and aggressively seeking to arrive at arms control agreements."

The message, however, that Kennedy and his advisors paid particular attention to, and underlined as they read, was the following sentence: *"Political history does not support that it is more dangerous to be strong than to be weak, more dangerous to threaten than to betray fear, more dangerous to be as 'provocative' as an Adenauer or a DeGaulle than to be as concilliatory as a Macmillan."*[5] Kennedy and his generation were the children of the New Deal. They witnessed the League of Nations' failure to halt Japanese aggression against Manchuria and Mussolini's conquest of Ethiopia. They were old enough to have served in World War II. They made their careers in the years of the Cold War and the threat of war had thus become part of their lives. The president and his advisors came away from these experiences having learned three lessons: the value of strong executive leadership; the need for collective security; and the necessity of military strength in foreign affairs.[6]

Khrushchev's Road to Power

Nikita Khrushchev was already one of the most powerful men in the Soviet Union when the Wehrmacht and the Red Army swept into Poland in September 1939. His journey to the Soviet pinnacle was meteoric. The son of a miner, Khrushchev rose from the coal pits of the Donbass to become Stalin's viceroy in the Ukraine. By the end of the year, he was firmly ensconced in Stalin's personal entourage as a voting member of the Politburo.

Khrushchev survived the war and Stalin's paranoia as well. In September 1953, six months after Stalin's death, Khrushchev became First Secretary of the Communist Party. During the next four years, he skillfully waged a determined struggle to dominate the Party and the governmental apparatus of the Soviet Union. Khrushchev showed a remarkable ability, in the midst of the succession struggle, to expropriate the policies of his defeated opponents.

Khrushchev's principal rival, Premier Georgi M. Malenkov, asserted in March 1954 that a new world war would lead to "the destruction of world civilization." Malenkov used the thermonuclear standoff to bolster his argument that more could be done to meet the economic demands of the long-suffering Soviet consumer without diminishing Soviet security. Ranged against this assertion were the military service chiefs, their supporters in heavy industry, and Khrushchev. Malenkov's initiative coincided with a closed debate within the defense establishment on the impact of nuclear weapons on the laws of war. He badly misjudged the strength of the modernizers in the military. Six weeks later, Malenkov conceded that a future war would spell the "end of the capitalistic system." Khrushchev's *volte-face* began with Malenkov's fall from power in February 1955. The following year, Khrushchev propounded his own heresies.

The Twentieth Party Congress marked a radical departure in the content and direction of Soviet politics. The delegates convened behind closed doors on February 27, 1956, to hear Khrushchev deliver his secret speech. The audience listened in rapt silence during the next two hours as Khrushchev presented a litany of Stalin's crimes against the Party and the Soviet people. The effect of the speech was devastating. Reports afterwards indicated that many of the delegates broke down and cried. In one case, the shock of the revelations proved fatal. Boreslaw Bierut, the Stalinist First Secretary of the Polish Communist Party, suffered a heart attack and died in Moscow.

Khrushchev's Central Committee report, given on the opening day of the congress, is central to understanding the strategy behind Khrushchev's radical revision of Soviet foreign policy. Khrushchev declared that a war between the capitalist and socialist states was no longer fatalistically inevitable. The speech was a clear acknowledgment of the new realities of contemporary international relations. The thermonuclear standoff had opened the possibilities for revolutionary action, and even local wars by proxy. But Khrushchev was exceedingly sensitive to the dangers of escalation once Soviet forces became engaged in a regional conflict. In fact, Khrushchev's subsequent distinction between "world wars, local wars, and liberation wars and popular uprisings" was a means of justifying Soviet abstention from direct military involvement while maintaining an ideologically correct position in support of wars of national liberation.[7] Ideological success obliged the Soviet Union to convince the bourgeois nationalists in the Third World that the U.S.S.R. was a strong and vibrant society, not the fountainhead of violent revolution.

In Isaac Deutscher's view, the proceedings "looked forward not to the seizure of new positions of power for Communism, but to the consolidation and building up of the power which Communism had already won."[8] Khrushchev realized that he needed to come to terms with the United States, and established a *modus vivendi*, if you will, in order to consolidate his control over the Sino-Soviet bloc. "The establishment of firm, friendly relations between the two largest powers of the world – the U.S.S.R. and the United States of America – would be of tremendous value in strengthening world peace." This accommodation, Khrushchev told the delegates, must be based on the five principles of peaceful coexistence: mutual respect for territorial integrity and sovereignty; non-aggression; non-interference in each other's internal affairs; equality and mutual benefit; and economic cooperation.[9] For this strategy to succeed, however, Khrushchev needed the West's affirmation of the Soviet Empire's postwar boundaries and American acceptance of the Soviet Union as an equal competitor on the world scene.

It's hardly surprising that Khrushchev's protestations of peace fell on deaf ears in the United States and Western Europe. The rhetoric of American foreign policy was peppered with sanctimonious demands for the liberation of Eastern Europe. The threat of Soviet aggression was considered to be no different than the Fascist onslaught of the 1930s. British and French cowardice at Munich was still a vivid memory for the statesmen of the North Atlantic Alliance. Any accommodation with Khrushchev, short of Soviet capitulation, smacked of appeasement to the architects of U.S. foreign policy — Dean Acheson and John Foster Dulles.

In June 1957 Khrushchev parried an attempt by a majority of the Party Praesidium to depose him with a vote of no confidence. A few weeks later, Khrushchev arrived at a Moscow diplomatic reception in an exuberant mood. Shortly afterwards, he related a fable to a group of Western journalists that revealed as much about his own personality as it did about the recent political turmoil in the Kremlin.

"Once upon a time," Khrushchev began, "there were three men in prison: a social democrat, an anarchist and a humble little Jew — a half-educated little fellow named Pinya. They decided to elect a cell leader to watch over the distribution of food, tea, and tobacco. The anarchist, a big, burly fellow, was against such a lawful process as electing authority. To show his contempt for law and order, he proposed that the semi-educated Jew, Pinya, be elected, and thus, Pinya became the cell leader.

"Things went well," Khrushchev continued, "and they decided to escape. But they realized that the first man to go through the tunnel would be shot by the guard. They all turned to the big, brave anarchist, but he was afraid to go. Suddenly poor little Pinya drew himself up and said, 'Comrades, you elected me by democratic process as your leader. Therefore, I will go first.'

"The moral of the story," Khrushchev explained, "is that no matter how humble a man's beginning, he achieves the stature of the office to which he is elected.

"That little Pinya," he concluded, "that's me."[10]

Nikita Khrushchev was never virtuous about his choice of tactics nor modest about his goals and expectations. He was a man of action, a dedicated Communist with the soul of a Russian peasant. At home, Khrushchev was ruthless with his opponents and openly solicitous for his proteges. Like Stalin, he mortgaged Soviet foreign policy to the growth of Soviet economic and military power. Unlike his patron, however, he was often too ready to parlay the perception of power to achieve his strategic objectives. Yet, throughout his tumultuous career, Khrushchev craved the respect of the world at large—especially the admiration of the United States. In the words of the Central Intelligence Agency's biographic sketch of Khrushchev, "...he has revealed an exaggerated sensitivity to imagined personal slights or reflections on his country's prestige while, on the other side, he takes great delight in private conversation in dropping the names of the world statesmen with whom he has corresponded or who have sent him gifts." Moreover, Khrushchev "feels that he ... and his nation, with which he has increasingly identified his own person, have acquired a station which entitles them to acceptance and respect, if not affection."[11]

During the months following the "Anti-Party Affair," Khrushchev angled for an opportunity to visit the United States. President Eisenhower's invitation did not materialize until July 1959, well after Khrushchev's abortive effort the previous fall to evict the Western powers from Berlin. Khrushchev arrived in Washington, D.C., on 15 September aboard a modern jet aircraft. He had no intention of experiencing once again the embarrassment of his arrival in Geneva in 1955 for his last summit. Khrushchev later recalled that moment with regret.

> Unfortunately, our own delegation found itself at a disadvantage from the very moment we landed.... The leaders of the other delegations arrived in four-engine planes and we arrived in a modest two-engine Ilyushin. Their planes were certainly more impressive than ours, and the comparison was somewhat embarrassing.[12]

The day after his arrival in Washington, Khrushchev attended a reception given in his honor by Senator J. William Fulbright, Chairman of the Senate Foreign Relations Committee. One of the members who met the Soviet leader was the junior senator from Massachusetts, John F. Kennedy. Kennedy later characterized Khrushchev as a "tough-minded, articulate, hard-reasoning spokesman for a system in which he was thoroughly versed and in which he thoroughly believed."[13] The Cold War was destined to take several dramatic turns for the worse before both men met again.

Immediately prior to the Camp David Summit, Isaac Deutscher set forth a series of maximum and minimum objectives behind Khrushchev's meeting with President Eisenhower. The actual record of the negotiations does not support his general line of speculation. Nevertheless, Deutscher did put his finger on several important themes that informed Khrushchev's foreign policy perspective. The first was Khrushchev's ultimate objective of a comprehensive political agreement based on a clear division of spheres of influence between NATO and the Soviet bloc. To a certain degree such a condominium of power had been a fact of the postwar world; but the United States and the Soviet Union had so far exercised it in mutual hostility. Khrushchev wanted to explore whether the Soviets and Americans could not possibly exercise it in mutual agreement—that is, preservation of the status quo in Europe and competitive penetration of Africa and Asia. The European status quo he envisioned, however, was unacceptable to NATO because it demanded the dissolution of Four Power control of Berlin and *de jure* recognition of the German Democratic Republic. Khrushchev's minimum goals were to keep the diplomatic pot boiling and to keep open prospects for future summits until the growth of Soviet economic and military power came into play to alter the international scene deeply and directly.[14]

Prelude to Paris

Khrushchev basked for the next several months in the political afterglow of his successful foray across America. Eisenhower's admission that the Berlin situation was "abnormal" proved to be a major coup for Khrushchev and lent credibility to his demands for a change in the city's political status. President Eisenhower looked forward to important gains in disarmament at the Paris Summit and even the possibility of a nuclear test ban agreement. Khrushchev had other plans in mind.

In a letter to Chancellor Konrad Adenauer, made public on February 2, 1960, Khrushchev confidently predicted that there were "grounds for definite hope that the Four Powers will reach a mutually acceptable solution of the Berlin problem" at the upcoming summit meeting.[15] Shortly after the disclosure of this letter, the Warsaw Pact's Political Consultative Committee met in Moscow to map a strategy for the Paris Summit. The final declaration praised the value of reciprocal visits by leaders of the opposing states, but sharply criticized the strengthening of NATO and the deployment of nuclear weapons in

West Germany, and accused Bonn of wanting to alter "the present frontiers established in Europe." All parties were urged to sign a German peace treaty, and in return the Warsaw Pact offered to sign a non-aggression pact with NATO.[16]

The following day, TASS reported that Khrushchev had met with Party boss Walter Ulbricht and Premier Otto Grotewald on 5 February to discuss "the future of the Soviet Union and the GDR with respect to the earliest conclusion of a peace treaty with Germany and the regularizing of the abnormal situation in West Berlin."[17] During an interview in Moscow with a correspondent from *Sovetskaya Rossiya*, Ulbricht stated that the GDR expected the summit meeting to establish a Four Power commission to draft a German peace treaty.[18]

The Soviet motives behind the 1958 Berlin Crisis, as well as Khrushchev's subsequent tactics on the German question, remain subject to various interpretations. For years, the Kremlin harbored the ambition of driving a wedge between the United States and its European allies. Sputnik gave rise to fears in the West that a "missile gap" was emerging in favor of the Soviets. Khrushchev may have believed that he could convert these concerns into tangible political gains. On the other hand, Khrushchev may have been motivated by his own visceral fear of a rearmed Germany. The United States had secured NATO's approval to station Thor and Jupiter missiles in Europe in response to Sputnik I. The Western Powers had adamantly refused to recognize East Germany, and they insisted on all–German free elections as a prelude to reunification. A Berlin settlement by "diktat" would be a major foreign policy triumph and eliminate the Russian nightmare of a hostile and united Germany armed with nuclear weapons. At the same time, Khrushchev could halt the hemorrhage of refugees leaving East Germany.

The U-2 Affair and the Paris Summit

May Day is the most important official holiday in the Soviet Union next to the annual celebration of the 1917 Revolution. The Soviet leadership ascends the steps of Lenin's mausoleum to watch a parade of Soviet military might and thousands of marchers proclaiming the economic and social miracles of the Soviet State. On the morning of May 1, 1960, Nikita Khrushchev and his colleagues experienced a far more telling demonstration of national power. At approximately 5:00 A.M., an American U-2 reconnaissance plane, piloted by

Francis Gary Powers, a contract employee of the CIA, left Pakistani airspace and crossed the Soviet border enroute to Bodo, Norway. Powers' mission was to photograph the Soviet missile test facilities at Tyuratam, Kapustin Yar, and Plesetsk. Approximately four hours into the flight, the U-2 was destroyed at an altitude in excess of 65,000 feet by a Soviet SA-2 surface-to-air missile. Powers ejected safely and was captured near Sverdlovsk, 1,200 miles inside Soviet territory.

American overflights of the Soviet Union by the U-2 had begun in 1956, and approximately thirty missions had been conducted during the next four years. As long as these flights remained secret, and the true state of the Soviet missile program concealed, Khrushchev could claim with impunity that the Soviet Union was militarily superior to the United States. Such claims offered several immediate benefits to Soviet foreign policy. First, they encouraged European conservative and socialist opinion to question the credibility of America's commitment to the defense of NATO. Simply stated, would the United States risk the destruction of American cities by Soviet missiles in the defense of Europe's capitals? Secondly, the image of Soviet military superiority gave credence to Khrushchev's assertion that the "correlation of forces" between capitalism and socialism had irrevocably shifted in Moscow's favor. Finally, Khrushchev's missile diplomacy probably gave pause to his domestic critics who doubted the wisdom of Khrushchev's economic and social reforms.

CIA Director Allen W. Dulles confirmed the loss of Powers' aircraft to the White House on 2 May. The National Aeronautics and Space Administration released a long-standing "cover" story to the press to the effect that an American weather plane had accidentally strayed into Soviet airspace and was missing. Eisenhower permitted the State Department to corroborate the NASA press release, despite Khrushchev's announcement on 5 May that the Soviet armed forces had destroyed an American spy plane.

Khrushchev stunned the administration on 8 May by stating that the U-2 had not only been shot down, but its pilot was captured and the wreckage was intact. The following day, Secretary of State Christian Herter admitted the U-2's espionage mission and justified the overflights on the grounds of protecting the U.S. and the Free World against a Soviet sneak attack. At an informal press conference in Moscow's Gorkiy Park, site of the wreckage display, Khrushchev threatened to shoot down any other U-2s that ventured across Soviet borders and to strike at their bases.

The Paris Summit opened on 16 May. Khrushchev spoke first, demanding an immediate apology from Eisenhower and the suspension of all future flights. Eisenhower refused to apologize, but he did assure Khrushchev that there would be no further U-2 flights over Soviet territory. Mr. Khrushchev responded by stalking out of the room.

The 1960 Presidential Campaign

Khrushchev cast his presidential ballot amidst the shambles of the Paris Summit. Shortly before his flight to East Berlin, Khrushchev told reporters, "There is a man with whom, if he were president, we could do business...; I am convinced of this. We remember the great Roosevelt...."[19] In Bucharest a few weeks later, Khrushchev was even more direct in his support for the Democratic nominee. "The Soviet people," he declared, "are naturally interested in the election of such a president and the formation of such a government that would understand and correct the mistakes made by the present U.S. government."[20] In Washington, Soviet Ambassador Mikhail Menshikov was actively soliciting the opinions of senior American officials about who the candidates might be and who their choices would be for Secretary of State.[21]

The Democrats and Republicans, of course, selected their standard bearers without much thought given to the Kremlin. John Kennedy promised his party and the electorate to get the country moving again. He blamed the Republicans and their candidate, Richard M. Nixon, for the decline in American prestige abroad, for economic stagnation at home, and for the parsimonious defense budgets that made the "missile gap" possible. In reality, the actual policy differences between the candidates were negligible. Nixon, however, was saddled with the unenviable task of explaining the advantages of four more years of Republican leadership.

Kennedy offered the vision of a bright future marked by economic prosperity and renewed respect overseas. He was absolutely confident that a combination of strong leadership and the expansion of U.S. military power would suffice to convince Premier Khrushchev to mend his erratic ways, renounce his ideological pretensions, and accede to a *Pax Americana*.

On the campaign stump, Kennedy claimed that

> The Communists have a strategy for world conquest and that
> strategy rests . . . on the use of every weapon of economic and ideo-
> logical conflict to win the allegiance of the uncommitted nations of
> the world and increase their dependence on the support of the

Soviet Union ... and on their belief that the United States lacks the will and the endurance to engage in a prolonged and difficult struggle for the protection of freedom. [He promised his listeners that, if he won the election, Khrushchev would face] in the sixties an America which is not only militarily strong but which is waging the offensive for freedom on all the many fronts of the Cold War.[22]

During the second nationally televised debate between the candidates on October 7, 1960, Kennedy outlined his prerequisites for a summit meeting with Khrushchev: "...before we go into the summit, before we ever meet again, I think it's important that the United States build its strength, that it build its military strength, as well as economic strength."[23]

Khrushchev arrived in New York in October, aboard the *Baltika*, with a delegation of Eastern European leaders in tow, to address the U.N. General Assembly. The visit was highlighted, of course, by Khrushchev banging his shoe to express his displeasure with the speaker at the podium. Khrushchev's petulance caused more than embarrassment: The Soviet delegation incurred a ten thousand dollar fine for its leader's "breach of procedure."[24] Before leaving New York, Khrushchev expressed his willingness to meet at the summit with the next president and his conviction that such a meeting would indeed take place despite the current political climate. Khrushchev emphasized his intention not to "advance any threats of any kind" in connection with Berlin.[25] On his return to Moscow, Khrushchev stated firmly that the question of a German peace treaty and Berlin had to be settled in 1961, and he proposed holding a post-election summit for this purpose.[26]

The Interregnum: November and December 1960

When the votes were tallied on 7 November, Kennedy received 49.7 percent and Nixon 49.6 percent, a difference of only 112,881 votes of the nearly 68.8 million votes cast. The next morning the president-elect awoke to find a message of congratulations from Nikita Khrushchev. Khrushchev was anxious to assure Kennedy that "there is no obstacle to maintaining and strengthening peace that cannot be overcome."[27] This was Khrushchev's opening gambit in pursuit of an early summit meeting.

On 11 November, Alexander Korneichuk, a Soviet playwright and reputed confidant of Khrushchev, met in New York City with W. Averell Harriman. The conversation was "blunt and frank," and

Korneichuk communicated Khrushchev's desire to make a "fresh start" in American-Soviet relations. When Korneichuk asked what might be done to improve relations, Harriman responded that the release of the two captured RB-47 crewmen was of "first importance."[28] The Soviets had shot down an American RB-47 bomber with six aboard in July over the Barents Sea. Since then, the two survivors had been languishing in a Soviet prison.

Three days later, Harriman met Ambassador Menshikov in Washington, at the Ambassador's request, to receive a message from Khrushchev. Khrushchev stated that he and his colleagues understood the need for anti–Soviet rhetoric in a campaign, but now "there must be some realistic way found to improve our mutual relations." Khrushchev restated the principal points of his recent telegram to Mr. Kennedy and hoped they "could follow the line of relations that existed during President Roosevelt's time, when Mr. Harriman was Ambassador." Harriman reiterated his belief that the Soviets should make a positive gesture by releasing the two airmen.[29]

Menshikov carried Khrushchev's message to Adlai Stevenson on 16 November. The Soviet premier was anxious to begin informal talks with official representatives of the new president. Khrushchev asked Stevenson to pass the word to Kennedy that the time was approaching when it would be "easier to reach an understanding [on a nuclear test ban] and that he has a sincere desire to do so." A disarmament agreement, Khrushchev contended, would "settle — basically — everything."[30]

Menshikov called on Harriman in New York City on 21 November with another message from Khrushchev. The Soviet premier was positively disposed to the release of the RB-47 survivors and he hoped that Kennedy would designate Harriman as his authoritative spokesman. Harriman told Menshikov that he believed that the president-elect would not authorize anyone to hold talks with the Soviets until he had assumed office, and then such authority would go to the Secretary of State.[31]

Menshikov met again with Harriman to present the key points from a lengthy memorandum sent by Khrushchev. The Soviet ambassador explained that Khrushchev wanted to begin informal talks as soon as possible. If these talks could be held away from the glare of publicity, they might prove useful to all concerned. Menshikov quoted Khrushchev as saying:

> We obviously have different ideologies, but we should attempt to keep these differences out of our relations. If they are accentuated,

it would lead to war. Peaceful coexistence means competition and, if possible, cooperation.[32]

Soviet pressure to achieve an accommodation with the administration intensified with the approach of Mr. Kennedy's inauguration. At a New Year's Day reception in Moscow, Khrushchev stated that the Soviet Union would drop the complaint it had lodged with the U.N. over the U-2 incident; he trusted that "a fresh wind will blow with the coming of the new president."[33]

The First Hundred Days

Kennedy's inaugural address of January 20, 1961, must have dismayed Khrushchev. On the one hand, the new president called on the Soviets to "begin anew the quest for peace, before the dark powers of destruction unleashed by science engulf all of humanity in planned or accidental self-destruction." Then he promptly warned the American people not to "tempt" the Communist powers "with weakness. . . . For only when our arms are sufficient beyond doubt can we be certain beyond doubt that they will never be employed."[34]

Khrushchev summoned Ambassador Llewellyn Thompson to the Kremlin the next day and gave him a message for Mr. Kennedy urging "business-like cooperation" and a "step-by-step approach" to resolve their mutual differences. An early summit, he said, would lead to a "radical improvement in relations between our two countries."[35] Thompson, however, was deeply troubled by Khrushchev's recent public remarks on the results of the Moscow conference of Communist parties held in November. Khrushchev described the current "epoch" as "a time of struggle between the two opposing social systems, a time of socialist revolution and national liberation, a time of the breakdown of imperialism, of the abolition of the colonial system, a time of transition of more people to the socialist path, of the triumph of socialism and communism on a world-wide scale." Khrushchev went on to speak of the "inevitability" of wars of national liberation. "The Communists support just wars of this kind wholeheartedly and without reservation."[36] Such rhetoric, Thompson told Khrushchev, led many in the West to believe that "the Soviet Union itself desired to dominate the world with Communism as a means to this end." Khrushchev vehemently denied the charge.[37] Thompson's own preliminary assessment of Khrushchev's speech noted that the address was replete with passages that clearly referred to Soviet difficulties

with the Chinese. He added, however, "if taken literally [the] statement is [a] declaration of Cold War."[38]

Ambassador Thompson provided a more comprehensive analysis
of Soviet political motives two weeks later. He argued that the key to
current Soviet foreign policy was Khrushchev's belief that "if he can
gain [a] period of reduction of tension and hopefully some diversion
[of] resources from armaments to productive purposes and possibly,
even aid in [the] form [of] credits and technology from the West, he
can lead [the] Soviet Union into [an] era [of] Communism and, by way
of example, set most of [the] rest of [the] world on [the] path toward
this goal." In the Embassy's judgment, Khrushchev had little choice
but to compromise with the Chinese at the November 1960 Moscow
meeting since Khrushchev could not demonstrate that there was any
possibility of accommodation with the West. Thompson cautioned the
administration not to treat the Communist threat as primarily military
in nature to the exclusion of its political dimension. Although the
Chinese polemics may have rejuvenated the revolutionary elan of the
Soviet Party, "even Soviet Communists have a strong strain of na-
tionalism." If Khrushchev could offer his people a period of tranquil-
ity, Thompson would not exclude the possibility of a complete break
between Moscow and Beijing.[39]

Some in the administration reacted with alacrity to the nascent
spirit of detente. Adlai Stevenson, the new U.S. Ambassador to the
United Nations, told reporters on 27 January that he thought Mr.
Kennedy would agree to meet Premier Khrushchev during the General
Assembly's special session on disarmament, scheduled to begin on 7
March. The White House Press Office promptly repudiated Stevenson's comment with a curt statement that he was expressing his "personal views."[40] The president himself was profoundly suspicious of
Khrushchev's motives. He sensed an obvious contradiction between
Khrushchev's desire for peace and friendship with the United States
and the Soviet leader's apparent unbridled support for wars of national liberation in the Third World. The president, like his predecessor, wanted the "real" Khrushchev to step forward. Revolution and
pragmatism, of course, were part and parcel of Khrushchev's political
psyche. Ambassador Thompson never failed to stress this point in his
cables. "When Khrushchev speaks as chief of state of his desire for
peaceful solutions, he [is] quite sincere and, therefore, effective. . . . At
the same time he has in his speech of 6 January frankly and bluntly
expressed his Communist beliefs and policies." Consequently, "we
both look at [the] same set [of] facts and see different things . . . this
complicates arriving at solutions."[41]

Years later, senior Soviet officials would tell their counterparts in the Kennedy Administration that it was all a mistake, the 6 January speech had been aimed not at the Americans, but at the Chinese.[42] President Kennedy ignored Khrushchev's conciliatory messages and seized upon the speech with enthusiasm. He ordered an analysis of the speech to be prepared and circulated among the fifty top officials in the government with instructions to "read, mark, learn and inwardly digest."[43] Secretary of Defense McNamara took the president at his word. The 6 January speech became an obligatory feature of his congressional testimony and public speeches during his first two years at the Pentagon. Kennedy himself took Khrushchev's rhetoric directly to the American people as justification for the expansion of U.S. military power. Addressing a Joint Session of Congress on the State of the Union ten days after his inauguration, Kennedy admonished his audience to "never be lulled into believing that either power [the Soviet Union or China] had yielded its ambitions for world domination forcefully restated only a short time ago."[44]

The Kennedy Administration did not begin its own review of Soviet-American relations until early February 1961. The press reported on 8 February that Ambassador Thompson was returning to the United States for consultations. The principal meeting took place three days later at the White House, attended by the president, Vice President Lyndon Johnson, Secretary of State Dean Rusk, Ambassador Thompson, and three of his predecessors: W. Averell Harriman, George F. Kennan, and Charles E. Bohlen.[45]

No firm decision was taken at the 11 February meeting on what message, if any, to send the Soviet leadership. Instead, the State Department and others were given five days to state their views and to respond to questions posed by the meeting's participants. State, for example, prepared a study of Sino-Soviet relations that was sent to McGeorge Bundy, the president's national security advisor, by Ambassador Bohlen on 16 February.[46] Kennedy received the same day a memorandum entitled *Some Possible Messages to Moscow* from W. Walt Rostow, a member of Bundy's staff. Rostow urged the president to "place the highest priority on protecting the truce lines which emerged from the Second World War." In a postscript, Rostow suggested that Kennedy might wish to write a letter to Khrushchev for Thompson to carry back.[47]

Kennedy accepted Rostow's idea, and Ambassador Thompson returned to the White House two days later to confer with the president and to finalize the letter to Khrushchev. The message reportedly contained three sections. The first stressed the importance of the

Geneva test ban negotiations and contained a preliminary discussion of the American proposal. The second section dealt with general disarmament and proposed a postponement of the disarmament talks until September 11, 1961. The final section was devoted to the offer of a personal, but informal, meeting between Kennedy and Khrushchev.[48]

This letter, along with virtually all of the other personal correspondence between both men, has never been made public. However, a letter from Harry Schwartz of the *New York Times* to Rostow on March 4, 1961, indicates that the Kennedy letter also contained a warning. Schwartz had met with Rostow on 2 March, and in his 4 March letter he enclosed "one result of the chat," a copy of a *Times* editorial of the same date. The editorial noted that Thompson's return to Moscow marked the beginning of "serious" diplomatic contacts between both sides. The outcome of these negotiations "will depend upon the attitude of Premier Khrushchev and his colleagues...." It was extremely important, the editorial went on to say, that "the Soviet Government realize that this is an interrelated world in which actions and policies exhibited in one area cannot help but influence actions and policies in another." The *Times* urged Khrushchev to introduce a "consistent line in Soviet policy.... [If not, he] runs the risk that he may force the Kennedy Administration to turn the vigor and imagination it is now applying to the task of trying to improve relations toward a less happy purpose." Schwartz confirmed that the editorial was a direct consequence of their previous chat, and he hoped that Dr. Rostow would find the editorial "drafted carefully enough to serve the intended purpose."[49]

Thompson arrived in Moscow on 2 March and immediately requested a meeting with Foreign Minister Andrei Gromyko. Khrushchev had no intention of speaking with Thompson and he promptly departed the next day for a whistle-stop tour of Western Siberia. Thompson caught up with Khrushchev a week later in Novosibirsk. The Soviet Premier was bitter and ill-tempered. He had lost interest in the test ban negotiations. He was hostile to the administration's request to delay the disarmament talks until the fall, and he truly resented the fact that his proposal for a formal summit meeting had been transformed into an informal get-together.

Kennedy presented his long-awaited special defense message on 15 March, along with a request to Congress for an additional $6 billion in supplemental appropriations. Six days later, Soviet Ambassador Semyon Tsarapkin withdrew the U.S.S.R.'s earlier agreement to name a single administrator for the proposed nuclear test ban control commission. Tsarapkin insisted that the commission must be run by a three-man executive, a *troika* representing the Western, Communist, and Neutralist blocs. The press reported on 23 March that Kennedy had ordered an immediate increase in aid for Laos to stem the Pathet Lao offensive on the Plain of Jars at the northern approaches to the capital, Vientiane. Three carrier task forces of the Seventh Fleet and a 1,400-man Marine unit were redeployed off the Indochinese coast.

One school of thought saw the last week in March 1961 as crucial to the subsequent deterioration in Soviet-American relations. Embittered by the murder of Congolese President Patrice Lumumba and the combativeness of the Kennedy Administration, the Soviets now set out to test the administration, remove Dag Hammarskjold as U.N. Secretary General, increase the political strains in NATO, and take the Americans to task in the Third World.[50] Soviet expectations for a rapprochement with the United States, however, had begun to wane in late February. On 16 February Soviet Ambassador Andrei Smirnov, who was expected to stay in Moscow on home leave for another month, reappeared in Bonn after a meeting with Khrushchev. The next day, Smirnov presented a lengthy *aide memoire* to Dr. Adenauer that reiterated the Soviet threat to sign a peace treaty with East Germany and settle the issue on its own terms.[51]

Khrushchev was interviewed by Walter Lippmann on April 10, 1961, and revealed that there was a strong possibility he and Kennedy would meet in Vienna or Stockholm.[52] In less than a week, the chances for a summit were in doubt. In the early morning hours of 16 April, 1,400 Cuban exiles, supplied and trained by the CIA, waded ashore at the Bay of Pigs. The invasion force was pinned on the beach moments after the landing began. The ships offshore carrying ammunition and communications gear were sunk on the first day. Castro immediately arrested 200,000 people in Havana suspected of underground activities, and the hopes of a national uprising evaporated. Khrushchev vigorously condemned the invasion and warned the United States that the Soviet Union would provide "the Cuban people and the government all necessary help to repel [an] armed attack on Cuba." Khrushchev failed to repeat his threat of the previous summer to defend Cuba with rockets, but the Kennedy Administration was just as disturbed by his veiled warning that ". . . any so-called 'little war' can touch off a chain reaction in all parts of the globe."[53]

Kennedy moved quickly to confront his domestic and foreign critics in the weeks after the fiasco. The president told the American Society of Newspaper Editors on 20 April that the United States faced a "relentless struggle in every corner of the globe that goes far beyond the clash of armies or even nuclear armaments." These weapons serve as a "shield behind which subversion, infiltration, and a host of other tactics steadily advance picking off vulnerable areas one by one in situations which do not permit our own armed intervention."[54] Speaking to the newspaper publishers the following week, Kennedy told his audience that America is ". . . opposed around the world by a monolithic and ruthless conspiracy that relies primarily on covert means for expanding its sphere of influence. . . . It is a system which has conscripted vast human and material resources into the building of a tightly knit, highly efficient machine. . . ."[55]

The president's rhetoric created consternation in some quarters of the administration. Ambassador Thompson urged Secretary Rusk, in an "Eyes Only" cable, to prevail upon Kennedy not to withdraw his invitation to meet with Khrushchev.[56] Kennedy did not have to be convinced.

> I have to show him that we can be just as tough as he is. I can't do that by sending messages to him through other people. I'll have to sit down with him, and let him see just who he's dealing with.[57]

The proposal remained dormant until early May, when Gromyko asked Thompson if Kennedy was still interested in the meeting. On 16 May Ambassador Menshikov called on the president to read him an English translation of a letter from Khrushchev dated 12 May in response to Kennedy's letter of 22 February. Three days later, the American and Soviet governments announced that Kennedy and Khrushchev would meet in Vienna on the third and fourth of June.[58]

The Vienna Summit

Paris was the first stop on President Kennedy's European itinerary. His visit to President Charles de Gaulle was more than a courtesy call for the sake of allied unity. Kennedy wanted the French president's advice and counsel before facing Khrushchev. The President believed that his primary task at Vienna was to convince Khrushchev that the West intended to oppose firmly his machinations over Germany and Berlin. If Khrushchev wanted war, de Gaulle told Kennedy, then Khrushchev must realize that he would have it the first moment he used force against the West. Khrushchev must be made to realize that fighting around Berlin would mean a world war. De Gaulle insisted, however, that war was the last thing that Khrushchev wanted.[59] In Paris, Kennedy received a special background paper prepared by the State Department that set the tone for his confrontation with the Soviet leader. The paper contended that "world peace cannot be preserved by an attempt to inflict political defeats upon great powers and our reciprocal actions should be governed by some form of ground rules in order to avoid the types of actions which can set off an automatic chain of events leading to the end that both countries desire to avoid." At the same time, "ideological topics or references to the general threat of communism in the world should not be dealt with per se but as a function of and in relation to Soviet state policy."[60] The paper correctly anticipated the dilemma confronting Kennedy, but it did not offer a reasonable solution.

The first meeting in Vienna took place on 3 June at the residence of the American ambassador. Both sides engaged in perfunctory pleasantries and both leaders expressed their peaceful intentions. Then Kennedy made a mistake. As Ambassador Bohlen reports, the president let Khrushchev draw him into an ideological discussion about Marxist theory, a subject that Khrushchev was a master at handling.[61] Kennedy told Khrushchev that the key issue both men faced was how two great powers could avoid a confrontation in a period of great social change. According to Arthur Schlesinger, Kennedy intended to propose a standstill in the Cold War so that neither the Soviet Union nor the United States would find itself committed to actions which would risk its essential security, threaten the existing balance of forces, or endanger world peace. The whole notion of miscalculation irritated Khrushchev. It was a vague term, he said, and it suggested to him that America wanted the Soviet Union to sit like a schoolboy with his hands on top of the desk. The Soviet Union would defend its vital interests, regardless of whether the United States regarded such acts as miscalculations.[67]

Two conflicting views of the international status quo stood at the core of this discussion. Kennedy believed that social change need not upset the approximate balance between both blocs. He looked forward to the emergence of nationalistic, albeit neutralist, regimes susceptible to being induced to follow a pro–American policy with aid and trade. Khrushchev, on the other hand, subscribed to, for lack of a better phrase, a dynamic status quo. This meant that the Western democracies had no right to interfere in the domestic politics of the Communist bloc, while the Communists had every right to intervene in the internal affairs of any other country.

Kennedy and Khrushchev were able to agree to use their influence to persuade their respective clients in Laos to cooperate with the International Control Commission and support a cease-fire. However, there was no progress on a comprehensive test ban treaty. Khrushchev refused to budge from his demand for a maximum of three inspections per year and insisted upon a *troika* instead of a single enforcement administrator.

The remainder of the summit was devoted to Berlin and Khrushchev's threat to sign a peace treaty with the GDR by the end of the year. Kennedy, however, was not about to let Khrushchev have the last word on the matter. As their last formal meeting began to wind down late in the afternoon on 4 June, the president balked. "No," he told his aides, "we're not going on time. I'm not going to leave until I know more." Both men went outside into the courtyard of the Soviet embassy, accompanied only by their interpreters. Khrushchev said again that his decision to sign the peace treaty was "firm" and "irrevocable." "If that is true," Kennedy said, "its going to be a cold winter."[63]

The popular perception of the Vienna Summit is one of a young, inexperienced Kennedy bullied by an arrogant Khrushchev. The source of the stories was Kennedy himself. According to Kenneth O'Donnell, the president's appointment secretary, Kennedy said:

> I'd like to get across to the people at home the seriousness of the situation, and the *New York Times* would be the place to do it. I'll give Scotty [James Reston] a grim picture. But actually as de Gaulle says, Khrushchev is bluffing and he'll never sign that treaty. Anybody who talks the way he did today, and really means it, would be crazy, and I'm sure he's not crazy.[64]

In Reston's account of the interview, "Kennedy came into a dim room in the American embassy shaken and angry." It was the "roughest" experience of his career, Kennedy said:

> I think he [Khrushchev] did it because of the Bay of Pigs. I think he thought that anyone who was so young and inexperienced as to get into that mess could be taken, and anyone who got into it and didn't see it through, had no guts. So he just beat hell out of me. So I've got a terrible problem. If he thinks I'm inexperienced and have no guts, until we remove those ideas we won't get anywhere with him.[65]

On his flight to London, Kennedy continued to manipulate the public perception of Vienna. According to O'Donnell, Kennedy took the occasion to express aloud to a few close associates the implications of Khrushchev's truculent attitude towards Berlin.

> If I'm going to threaten Russia with nuclear war, it will have to be for much bigger and more important reasons than [Berlin]. Before

I back Khrushchev against the wall and put him to a final test, the freedom of all of Western Europe will have to be at stake.[66]

Joseph Alsop quoted an additional part of Kennedy's soliloquy and drew a different conclusion. "If you could think of only yourself," Kennedy remarked, "it would be easy to say you'd press the button, and easy to press it, too." When you think of the next generation, "that makes it damn hard." According to Alsop's sources, Kennedy concluded that it was a choice that might have to be made. Back in Washington, Alsop tells us, the president "got out" the Eisenhower Administration's studies of the potential casualties in a nuclear exchange.[67]

The Berlin Cauldron

Khrushchev addressed the Soviet people on 21 June wearing the uniform and shoulder boards of a lieutenant general, his rank as a political commissar during World War II. "Everyone knows that we do not want war," Khrushchev declared, "but if you really threaten us with war, we are not afraid of such a threat . . . this will mean suicide for you."[68] On 8 July Khrushchev announced a halt to planned troop reductions in 1961 and an increase in defense spending from 3.14 billion rubles to 12.4 billion rubles. In this same speech (to military academy graduates in Moscow), Khrushchev expressed one of the more important Soviet motives behind the 1961 Berlin crisis: "With equal strength, there must be equal rights and equal opportunities."[69] The day after, the Soviets staged a massive display of air power for the first time since 1956 at the Tushino Air Field near Moscow. Four new fighter interceptors and two new long-range bombers were unveiled.

In Washington, an intense bureaucratic battle was in progress. President Kennedy had previously commissioned former Secretary of State Dean Acheson to prepare a report on the Berlin problem. The Acheson report concluded that the primary reason the Soviets wanted to alter the status of Berlin was to neutralize Germany and fragment NATO. The report recommended a series of NATO mobilization measures, close consultations with the allies in Europe, especially West Germany, and the declaration of a national emergency in the event access to West Berlin was denied. The report also included a sequence of military operations, culminating in a two-division probe down the Helmstadt autobahn to break a future blockade. By July, the bureaucratic battle lines were drawn between supporters and opponents of the Acheson report. The latter faction was more inclined to use traditional diplomacy to defuse the crisis. Both groups, however, were united on the defense of three critical American interests in West Berlin: unrestricted access, the right to maintain a military garrison, and the continued economic and political viability of the city.[70]

The president met with his Joint Chiefs of Staff and the National Security Council on 19 July to finalize U.S. policy towards Berlin, and, the following evening, Mr. Kennedy addressed the nation. The president stated that the Western presence and access to Berlin could not be ended by Soviet fiat.

> The NATO shield was long ago extended to cover West Berlin — and we have given our word that an attack upon the city will be regarded as an attack on us all. . . . We need the capability of placing in any critical area at the appropriate time a force which, with our allies, is large enough to make clear our determination and our ability to defend our rights at all costs — and to meet all levels of aggressor pressure with whatever levels of force are required. . . . We intend to have a wider choice than humiliation or all-out nuclear war.

Kennedy requested $3.247 billion in additional defense appropriations. Some $1.8 billion was devoted to the procurement of equipment and ammunition. Draft calls would be increased, and selective reserve units activated. Kennedy also called for increased attention to civil defense. "In the event of attack," he stated, "the lives of those families which are not hit in a nuclear blast and fire can still be saved — if they can be warned to take shelter and if that shelter is available."[71]

The Soviet press immediately accused the Kennedy Administration of "war drum beating and hysteria." Khrushchev received news of this speech as he was conferring in Sochi with John J. McCloy, the U.S. disarmament negotiator, and immediately flew into a "foot-stomping, bellowing rage." Khrushchev told McCloy that he was considering production of a 100-megaton bomb.[72]

Italian Premier Amintore Fanfani and Foreign Minister Antonio Segni arrived in Moscow on 2 August for a state visit. Khrushchev told them that, if war came over Berlin, it would be a nuclear war from the beginning. He repeated this about twelve times during the talks. He kept saying that this was not a threat but he had no other choice. At one point, Khrushchev drew a crude map and told Fanfani that the first two countries to be destroyed in a war would be Italy and Great

Britain because each contained many bases with missiles aimed at the Soviet Union. He also told his guests that he was under pressure to begin testing a 100-megaton weapon.[73]

The stream of refugees into West Berlin now threatened to become a flood. During the first twelve days of July, over 8,000 people fled to the Western sectors, and by 13 August, they were arriving at a rate of over a thousand per day.

Ambassador Menshikov sailed for home on 20 July. Ten days later, Ambassador Smirnov in Bonn was recalled to Moscow. Presumably, Khrushchev wanted to consult with his two principal ambassadors before sealing off the Eastern sector of the city. He evidently reached his decision sometime between 31 July and 2 August. The Party first secretaries of the other Warsaw Pact nations arrived in Moscow on 2 August. A subsequent CIA report indicated that the Polish delegation persuaded the Soviets and East Germans to lift their deadline for a peace treaty once the wall was in place.[74]

With the decision reached, Khrushchev attempted to ease the crisis. On 7 August Khrushchev stated that a "clash would have the most disastrous consequences for everyone."[75] Khrushchev reached for the "war hysteria" theme in an address four days later:

> There must be a sense of proportion and military passions must not be fanned. If the feelings are let loose and they predominate over reason, then the fly wheel of war preparations can start revolving at a high speed. Even when reason prompts that a brake should be put on, the fly wheel of war preparations may have acquired such speed and momentum that even those who had set it revolving will be unable to stop it.[76]

Ulbricht announced on 10 August that the GDR had decided to take measures to stop the "traffic in human beings." The same day, the East German news agency disclosed that Marshal Ivan Konev had assumed command of the Soviet forces in East Germany. The sector border was closed during the early morning hours of August 13, 1961. Simultaneously, the GDR assured Bonn that these "measures" would not affect the existing controls on traffic between West Berlin and the Federal Republic.[77]

The American protest was not lodged until 17 August. Kennedy followed this up by sending a convoy with 1,500 American troops down the autobahn, and he dispatched Vice President Johnson and General Lucius Clay, the hero of the 1948 Berlin airlift, to demonstrate the American commitment to the city's freedom.

During the next two weeks, a series of reciprocal military measures took place. On 14 August two Soviet army divisions moved into position around Berlin. Shortly afterwards, the Pentagon ordered 76,500 reservists to active duty.

On August 31, 1961, the Soviet Union announced its resumption of nuclear testing; the first shot of the series was detonated almost immediately near Semipalitinsk in Soviet Central Asia. Kennedy and Prime Minister Harold Macmillan sent a joint letter to Khrushchev on 3 September asking for a cessation of the Soviet test series. Moscow rejected the request two days later and Kennedy immediately approved the resumption of U.S. underground nuclear tests. Khrushchev formally replied to the letter on 9 September and demanded a German peace treaty in exchange for a cessation of the Soviet tests. The following day, the Soviets announced a series of long-range rocket tests in the Pacific to be conducted between 13 September and 15 October.

Kennedy received a confidential letter from Khrushchev on 29 September indicating his willingness to resume negotiations on Berlin. Three weeks later, Khrushchev told the delegates to the Twenty-Second Communist Party Congress that a German peace treaty would no longer have to be signed by the end of the year.

Motives and Expectations

General Lyman Lemnitzer, the Chairman of the Joint Chiefs of Staff, claimed that the construction of the Berlin Wall came as a complete surprise to the administration.[78] NATO contingency plans, for example, expected the Soviets to follow a scenario similar to the 1948 crisis. President Kennedy, however, learned that the Soviets and East Germans intended to block free access between East and West Berlin at least one week before the wall appeared. Kennedy told Walt Rostow that there was not a "damn thing" the West could do about it. The president conceded that unless Khrushchev halted the drain of people through West Berlin, Soviet domination of Eastern Europe would crumble. Kennedy was prepared to go to war to defend West Berlin, but he was not ready to liberate East Berlin.[79] When a reporter later asked the president to explain his reluctance to tear down the wall, Kennedy replied: "I think that you could have had a very violent reaction which might have taken us down a very rocky road, and I think it was that reason ... that no recommendation was made ... at that time."[80] Khrushchev was equally forthright in his memoirs about the purpose of the Berlin Wall. "Unfortunately, the GDR—not only the

GDR—has yet to reach a level of moral and material development where competition with the West is possible."[81] In other words, Communist dominoes from Berlin to Moscow would also fall, if the contagion of freedom toppled the Ulbricht regime.

The Berlin Wall was a crude but effective response to the threat of political instability in Eastern Europe. However, Khrushchev considered a German peace treaty to be no less important. The treaty would legitimize the postwar boundaries of the Soviet Union, Czechoslovakia, and Poland as well as the political division between East and West. Moreover, Khrushchev expected the treaty to codify the Soviet Union's status as a superpower. In his words,

> That is why the question of the fight for a peace treaty with Germany is not only literally for a peace treaty.... This is a question of our fight for the recognition of our grandeur.[82]

Foreign Minister Gromyko expressed this sentiment even more explicitly during his own speech to the Twenty-Second Party Congress on October 27, 1961. In Gromyko's words, the Soviet Union "attaches special importance to the state of relations between the two giants, the Soviet Union and the United States of America.... After all, if these two powers combined their efforts in safeguarding peace, who would dare to and who would be able to break it? No one."[83] Gromyko clearly had the threat of German revanchism in mind, and he seemed to be saying, "What better way to keep Adenauer and Ulbricht in line than with a Soviet-American condominium?" Three months later, a senior Soviet specialist in international affairs called for a "platform of collaboration" with the West to prevent thermonuclear war and facilitate economic progress.[84]

The Kennedy Administration had neither the interest nor the inclination to fashion a political accommodation with Khrushchev. Khrushchev's proposals on Berlin and Germany conveyed to them the real danger of Soviet expansionism. In fact, the administration grossly misperceived Khrushchev's objective of bolstering the legitimacy and stability of the Soviet Bloc. In Washington, Assistant Secretary of Defense Paul Nitze told the Association of the United States Army that Berlin was "merely a proving ground" to "demonstrate our impotence in the face of the much advertised Soviet power," and to impose a "psychological defeat" on the West. Khrushchev was following "salami tactics," according to Nitze, to force a series of Western withdrawals, no one of which was sufficient to cause a war.[85]

The implicit historical parallel to the 1930s is difficult to ignore in

Nitze's remarks. Twenty years earlier, John Kennedy had written eloquently about the absolute necessity of a democratic "armed guard" to deter the "fire" of totalitarian aggression. Khrushchev's threat to Berlin was no different, in the administration's opinion, from Hitler's aggression. The principal question was how to convince Khrushchev that the U.S. would fight rather than allow the destruction of West Berlin's freedom and the dismemberment of NATO. This question completely overshadowed the negotiable issues of German boundaries, *de facto* recognition of the GDR, and the Federal Republic's future armaments.[86] The preeminent objective was to ensure that Khrushchev did not miscalculate U.S. resolve to defend its European commitments. In Nitze's words, the U.S. would back these commitments with conventional capabilities and "by the use of our strategic capabilities should that be necessary."[87]

Once the deadline crisis passed, however, the administration pressed its psychological advantage against Khrushchev. Senior administration officials reminded the Soviets at every turn of the power and breadth of America's conventional and nuclear arsenal. The political objective of this campaign was to demonstrate that the U.S. could enforce the containment of the Soviet Union by military power alone. The rhetoric humiliated the Soviets. Khrushchev's retreat from the German peace treaty had severely constrained his foreign policy options. Politically, he could not afford the opprobrium of strategic inferiority. Khrushchev had no guarantee that the U.S. would respect Soviet vital interests without some semblance of strategic deterrence. The Soviets responded with missiles in Cuba.

The complexities of the Cuban missile crisis will be treated in greater detail in Chapter 6. Nevertheless, the evidence indicates that the crisis was symptomatic of a mutual misperception of Soviet and American strategic objectives. The causes of this distortion go far to explain the reasons for the crisis atmosphere that enveloped the superpowers between January 1961 and October 1962. On the American side, President Kennedy and his immediate advisors filtered Khrushchev's rhetoric and Soviet foreign policy behavior through the lens of the Munich experience. There was no appreciation of the fundamental conservatism of Khrushchev's strategy nor of his intense drive to secure for his nation the respect of the United States. The Munich syndrome impeded the administration's ability to recognize and exploit the diplomatic opportunity created by the Sino-Soviet conflict. Their attempt to reinforce the truce lines of the Cold War conformed with the view that the Soviets and Communist Chinese presented a united front against American interests abroad. Nuclear deterrence, predicated upon U.S. military superiority, was clearly an attractive strategy.

Not surprisingly, Khrushchev's conception of nuclear deterrence was in line with his attempts to consolidate the Soviet hold on Eastern Europe and invigorate the Soviet national economy. Khrushchev was satisfied with less than absolute parity as long as he could point to some semblance of mutual nuclear deterrence. Missiles, Khrushchev once told reporters, are not "cucumbers, they cannot be eaten, and to repel aggression one does not need more than a certain number of them."[88] He never realized, however, that in baiting the Eisenhower Administration with the "missile gap," he had sowed the seeds for an American response.

Khrushchev's conscious attempt to deceive the United States only stoked Washington's sense of danger. If the estimates of Soviet missiles that appeared in the American press in 1959 had been even partially correct, the dangers of Soviet political blackmail would have undoubtedly increased. By February 1961, however, the Kennedy Administration knew that the estimates of Soviet ICBM deployments were grossly inflated. Rather than striving to reduce Cold War tensions, President Kennedy orchestrated an unprecedented expansion in U.S. military power. Ironically, however, the United States was no more secure than it was before, and the Soviets had every incentive to restore the strategic balance.

Chapter 2

The Strategists:
McNamara and Malinovskiy

Our forefathers defeated our enemies without ever suspecting that
such a thing as military doctrine existed.
                                    Colonel-General S. Shtemenko

Personalities and Perspectives

Robert McNamara's appointment as Secretary of Defense had
more to do with his reputation for managerial brilliance than it did with
his strategic outlook. McNamara's technocratic style meshed well with
John Kennedy's intention to reform the operation of the Defense Department and alter the tenor of American military thinking. A Phi
Beta Kappa graduate of the University of California and a former
assistant professor at the Harvard Business School, McNamara re-
signed as president of the Ford Motor Company to become Secretary
of Defense. During World War II, he served in the Army Air Corps
as a statistical accountant and unraveled several logistical nightmares
that were hampering U.S. bomber operations in Europe and the Pacific. After the war, Henry Ford II recruited McNamara and several
other veterans of wartime operations research to join Ford Motors
and restore the company's profit margin. The cumulative success of
McNamara's efforts led to increasingly responsible executive assign-
ments at Ford during the next fourteen years. From McNamara's perspective, the techniques used to manage a corporate enterprise were no
different from those needed to administer a government agency. Organizational efficiency demanded a rational approach to decision making, and McNamara was a pioneer in the field of quantitative management.

Mr. Kennedy outlined his views on national defense in a review
he published during the campaign of B.H. Liddell Hart's book

Deterrent or Defense. Since the end of the Second World War, Kennedy observed, the United States has had to cope with "limited aggression by limited means." Yet at the same time, the Eisenhower Administration permitted U.S. conventional capabilities to atrophy. Kennedy went on to charge that "we have no right to tempt Soviet planners and political leaders with the possibility of catching our aircraft and unprotected missiles on the ground in a gigantic Pearl Harbor."[1] Once in the oval office, Kennedy hastened to improve the nation's ability to deter both contingencies. He ordered the Defense Department immediately to increase U.S. airlift capabilities and the procurement rate of Polaris submarines. The less obvious flaws in U.S. defenses were of equal concern. "The lack of consistent, coherent military strategy, the absence of basic assumptions about our national requirements and the faulty estimates and duplication arising from interservice rivalries," he complained in his first State of the Union address, "made it difficult to assess accurately how adequate or inadequate our defenses really are."[2] McNamara responded with firm leadership and a bureaucratic hammer: PPBS.

The "Planning-Programming-Budgetary-System" became the cutting edge of McNamara's efforts to recast American defense policy. The architect of this analytic process was Dr. Charles Hitch, an economist with the Rand Corporation who left the Santa Monica think-tank to become the Pentagon's comptroller during the McNamara years. The primary purpose of PPBS was to end the fierce interservice competition for dollars and prestige that had riddled the U.S. defense establishment since 1945. PPBS relied upon three conceptual tools. The computer models of operations research were used to determine the performance of competitive weapon designs under simulated combat conditions. These choices, in turn, were evaluated according to their relative cost effectiveness to insure maximum military output for each dollar spent. Finally, the techniques of systems analysis were used to relate weapons and forces to strategic or military needs. As a result, the entire defense budget was revamped according to program elements that crosscut service boundaries. For example, the costs of the Air Force's ICBMs, the Navy's SLBMs and the Army's BMD research were consolidated under the heading "Strategic Retaliatory Forces" in the DOD budget requests rather than entered as separate lines. The service secretaries and chiefs of staff were now required to justify their budgets on the basis of comparative costs and performance. However, the seeds of McNamara's revolution had already been planted in the late 1940s and early 1950s by a pattern of congressional irritation over the politics rampant in the Defense Department and executive willingness to promote to even greater authority the office of the Secretary of Defense.[3]

According to one member of Kennedy's inner circle, McNamara regarded himself not as an initiator of defense policy but as an engineer and expeditor of whatever defense policy the president chose to follow.[4] Calculated understatement was certainly part of McNamara's managerial repertoire, but his own goals were not limited to the organizational reform of the Defense Department. McNamara conceived his cabinet post as a "bully pulpit" to educate the American public about the realities of the nuclear era and to lecture the Soviets about what they should do to contribute to strategic stability.[5]

Nearly ten years older than McNamara, Rodion Malinovskiy was a hardened combat veteran with a military career spanning over four decades. He had the broadest foreign exposure of any of his contemporaries in the Soviet High Command, having fought in France, Germany, Spain, Rumania, Hungary, Austria, and Manchuria. At the age of sixteen, he joined the Imperial Army and served in France during World War I as a junior non-commissioned officer with the Czar's expeditionary force and later with the French Foreign Legion. Returning to Russia in 1919, he enlisted in the Red Army and fought against Admiral Kolchak's forces in Siberia as a junior officer with the First Horse Cavalry. In the early 1930s, Malinovskiy attended the Frunze Academy, the Red Army's staff college in Moscow. From January 1937 until June 1938, he was assigned as an advisor to Republican troops in Spain. During the Second World War, Malinovskiy led the Second Ukrainian Front, and his troops were responsible for the liberation of Bucharest, Budapest, and Vienna. Following the German surrender, Malinovskiy was transferred to the Soviet Far East and took command of the Transbaikal *Front*. The Soviet Union declared war on Japan on August 8, 1945, and Malinovskiy began his attack against the Kwantung Army in Manchuria the next day. Soviet armored columns covered 700 miles in five days and their victory made possible the eventual establishment of Communist power in China and North Korea. Malinovskiy remained in the Soviet Far East until his promotion in 1956 to First Deputy Minister of Defense and Commander-in-Chief of the Ground Forces, replacing Marshal I.S. Konev, who retained his command of the Warsaw Pact forces. Malinovskiy then succeeded Marshal Zhukov as Minister of Defense in October 1957.

Malinovskiy was a practitioner of military strategy, not a theoretician. To Walter Jacobs, Malinovskiy was "little more than a competent soldier who is willing to lend himself to the will of the politicians who may at any time be in power in the Soviet Union."[6] Admittedly, Malinovskiy's writings lacked the originality of those of some of his predecessors. However, Malinovskiy certainly played a particularly important role in the debates on military strategy that engaged the Soviet military and political elites during the early 1960s. Thomas Wolfe correctly notes that Malinovskiy was limited in his ability to show any independence of thought. He was beholden to Khrushchev for his job, and he realized, no doubt, that a repetition of Marshal Zhukov's boldness could be costly. Instead, Malinovskiy appears to have acted as a mediator in the debate. In Wolfe's opinion, Malinovskiy "sought to reconcile the general thrust of Khrushchev's views with the reservations probably felt by a substantial body of conservative opinion within the military."[7]

The Strategic Prologue

Military thought on both sides of the Iron Curtain was slow to discern the revolutionary import of nuclear weapons. Few believed that the character of a new world war would differ much from its predecessor. In Great Britain Professor P.M.S. Blackett argued that "a long-range [atomic] bombing offensive against a large continental Power is not likely to be by itself decisive within the next 5 years." Blackett's American counterpart, Professor Vannevar Bush, suggested that World War III would be a "contest of the old form, with variations and new techniques of one sort or another," including greater use of the atomic bomb.[8]

Stalin's view of war differed little from the outlook of Blackett and Bush. The year after the German invasion, Stalin promulgated a dictum that became the last word in Soviet military doctrine for the next ten years. Stalin decreed that victory on future battlefields would be determined by the side that capitalized upon what he termed the "permanently operating factors" of war. These factors included "the stability of the rear, the morale of the army, the quantity and quality of divisions, the armament of the army, [and] the organizational ability of the army commanders." Stalin dismissed the value of surprise and concluded that wars of the future, like those of the past, would be fought by land armies engaged in massive counteroffensive campaigns.[9]

Stalin's obstinate refusal to modify this dogma merits attention. The most obvious explanation is that any affirmation of the principle of surprise would have placed the Soviet Union's own lack of preparedness in 1941 under embarrassing scrutiny. Secondly, an admission of the revolutionary nature of atomic weapons, at a time when the United States possessed a nuclear monopoly, would have accentuated the Soviet Union's own nuclear inferiority. Finally, such an admission would have denigrated the coercive value of the Soviet armies poised at the frontiers of Western Europe.

The turning point in contemporary strategic thought occurred in 1953. The United States detonated its first thermonuclear device in December 1952, and the Soviets exploded their own hydrogen bomb in August 1953. The hydrogen bomb represented a quantum leap in the destructive force of nuclear energy. The power of these weapons was no longer calculated in the hundreds of tons of TNT but in the millions of tons. In destructive potential alone, a balance of terror had been achieved. The Eisenhower Administration, frustrated by the pointless protraction of the Korean War, and in search of a simple way to reduce defense expenditures and balance the federal budget, hastened to embrace the thermonuclear option.

Massive Retaliation and Its Critics

The first public expression of the Eisenhower Administration's so-called "New Look" in defense policy came in a speech by Secretary of State John Foster Dulles to the Council on Foreign Relations on January 14, 1954. Dulles announced that "local defense must be reinforced by the future deterrent of massive retaliatory power." Henceforth, the United States would "depend primarily upon a great capacity to retaliate instantly, by means and at places of our own choosing."[10] The hue and cry following Dulles' address prompted the administration's hasty withdrawal from an absolute interpretation of the doctrine. Five months later, the Secretary of State acknowledged the need for a "wide variety of means" to respond to aggression, and he vehemently denied that the strategy of massive retaliation meant "turning every local war into a world war."[11]

The doctrine of massive retaliation, combined with the administration's drastic budget cuts in conventional forces, sparked a wide-ranging debate among defense intellectuals in the United States. The critics tended to be academics, principally historians and political scientists, who were less concerned with the technical details of defense than with the perceived need to bring America's military power in line with its diplomatic commitments. They proposed a strategy of multiple options.[12] The President of the United States, they argued, should have an alternative other than appeasement or nuclear bombardment when confronted with local aggression. Two major studies appeared in 1956 which synthesized the theoretical premises of limited war: Henry Kissinger's *Nuclear Weapons and Foreign Policy* and Robert Osgood's *Limited War*. The thesis of both works was that a nuclear stalemate existed between the United States and the Soviet Union. Under these circumstances, massive retaliation would be unable to deter Communist terror, subversion, and insurgencies in contested parts of the world. The Eisenhower Administration's reluctance to use atomic weapons in 1954 to lift the siege at Dienbienphu and save the surrounded French garrison was taken by critics as proof of this proposition.

The successful launch of a Soviet intercontinental ballistic missile in August 1957 imparted a new sense of urgency to the discussion of military strategy in the United States. For the first time in its history, the continental United States was vulnerable to sudden attack. The technical characteristics of the strategic equation now drew increased attention. In a notable article in *Foreign Affairs*, Albert Wholstetter contended that a stable strategic balance demanded the ability to strike second; in other words, a secure retaliatory force. "A protected retaliatory capability has a stabilizing influence not only in deterring rational attack, but also in offering every inducement to both powers to reduce the chances of accidental war."[13]

The concept of a "stable balance" was also central to the work of Bernard Brodie. In an essay written a few months after the bombing of Hiroshima and Nagasaki, Brodie argued that atomic weapons vitiated the traditional value of victory in war.

> The first and most vital step in ... the age of atomic bombs is to take measures to guarantee to ourselves in case of attack the possibility of retaliation in kind. The writer in making the statement is not for the moment concerned about who will win the next war in which atomic bombs have been used. Thus far the chief purpose of our military establishment has been to win wars. From now on its chief purpose must be to avert them. It can have almost no other useful purpose.[14]

For Brodie, war in the nuclear era was bereft of any rational purpose. The costs to both sides would be so high in an atomic war as to outweigh any political gain. The key to deterrence, according to Brodie, was to guarantee the fear of retaliation. "If [an attacker] must fear retaliation, the fact that it destroys its opponents' cities some hours or even days before its own are destroyed may avail it little...."[15]

Brodie refined these themes in his book *Strategy in the Missiles Age*, published in 1959. In order for nuclear deterrence to succeed, Brodie argued, the "enemy must expect us to be vindictive and irrational if he attacks us. . . . We must give [the enemy] every reason to feel that that portion of our retaliatory force which survives his attack will surely be directed against his major population centers."[16] Brodie readily admitted that his book gave "relatively little space to the matter of how to fight a general nuclear war if it should come." He would go no further than to acknowledge the necessity of "appropriate precautions" if deterrence failed. Even with some semblance of civil defense, Brodie predicted that survival, in a post-attack world, would be a "grim prospect."[17]

With the exception of Herman Kahn's convoluted tome *On Thermonuclear War*, few American strategic analysts considered the problem of how to fight and win a thermonuclear war. The overwhelming majority stopped at the brink and, like Brodie, expounded a force posture of minimum deterrence, i.e., the capability to cause maximum civilian casualties with a minimum number of weapons. Taking Brodie's analysis to task, Kahn retorted that to ignore the prospect of nuclear war and simply rely upon the threat of mutual annihilation was naive at best, and at worst suicidal:

> *If our nation can survive the actual attack, and has made some minimal preparations, then in all probability, "the survivors will not envy the dead. . . ." Under these circumstances, in addition to having a deterrent capability, we might want an ability to actually fight and survive a war.*[18]

The central theme in Kahn's book was the limitation of damage of nuclear war, either by defensive preparations or by coercion. Kahn found it difficult to imagine "an enemy attack that could set us back economically to pre–World War I standards just by destroying physical assets," if there were stockpiles of basic necessities, fallout shelters and a reasonable air defense system. Even if one hundred metropolitan areas were destroyed in the United States during a nuclear exchange, Kahn asserted, "there would be more wealth in the country than there is in all of Russia today, and more skills than were available to that country in the forties."[19]

The other half of Kahn's damage limitation scheme was the use of coercion for what he called "controlled reprisal." The purpose of this strategy was to extend some modicum of deterrence into the period following a nuclear exchange "by using the threat of reprisal or escalation to induce the other side to avoid . . . collateral damage." In other words, Kahn envisaged a series of "tit-for-tat attacks" in which the "object is not the destruction of the other side's military power but the destruction of his resolve."[20] Kahn was not interested in victory as such, but rather the termination of hostilities short of defeat.

The Brodie and Kahn arguments accurately describe the strategic menu that confronted McNamara at the onset of his incumbency. He dallied momentarily with Kahn's notions of damage limitation. In the aftermath of the Cuban missile crisis, however, McNamara co-opted Brodie's rhetoric and called the strategy "assured destruction."

The McNamara Strategy

Robert McNamara was presented with a choice between two fundamentally different approaches to the problem of nuclear deterrence upon his arrival at the Pentagon. The senior leadership of the Navy, along with some support from the Army, favored a strategy of minimum deterrence. The Air Force, on the other hand, championed a so-called optimum approach to deterrence that resembled a first-strike strategy in all but name. The minimum deterrent option was a purely retaliatory strategy that relied upon a comparatively small number of Polaris submarines to decimate the urban and industrial centers of the Communist bloc. The Air Force's optimum strategy called for the procurement of a large and diversified force composed of land-based ballistic missiles and long-range bombers capable of crushing Soviet society and Soviet strategic nuclear attack forces in one great spasm of destruction. Neither alternative was very attractive to President Kennedy and his Secretary of Defense. A minimum deterrent might release funds for other purposes, but it offered the president only two choices: punitive retaliation or surrender. The optimum strategy had the advantage of forcing the opponent to decide whether or not to use nuclear weapons. Paradoxically, it also increased the enemy's incentive to launch a preemptive attack on his own. Both strategies contributed to deterrence. Neither option, however, contributed to the stability of the strategic balance.

McNamara took the advantages of each and fashioned them into a strategy of assured retaliation. President Kennedy outlined the details of the strategy in his March 1961 special message to Congress on defense. Kennedy insisted that these "[strategic] weapon systems must be usable in a manner permitting deliberation and discrimination as to timing, scope and targets in response to civilian authority." In addition, he demanded that these forces "must be designed to reduce the danger of irrational or unpremeditated general war, the dangers of an unnecessary escalation of a small war into a larger one, or miscalculation or misinterpretation of an incident or enemy intention."[21] The fulfillment of these requirements was contingent upon commensurate improvements in the command, control and communications network that links the president, or more precisely, the National Command Authority to the deployed forces.

Command, Control, and Communications

The Kennedy Administration inherited a substantial array of early warning capabilities constructed during the Eisenhower years. A ballistic missile early warning system, comprised of three large radar complexes at Clear, Alaska; Thule, Greenland; and Fylingdales Moor, Scotland, provided Washington with fifteen minutes of advanced warning of a Soviet ICBM attack. The Defense Early Warning network of radars, or DEW Line, spanning the Canadian Arctic, offered thirty minutes of warning in advance of a Soviet bomber attack against North America. The Semi-Automated Ground Environment system, SAGE for short, was the largest data processing system ever devised at the time. Using digital computers, SAGE coordinated the operations of fighter interceptors and air defense missiles with incoming radar warning data. The Sound Surveillance or SOSUS system tracked the movements of Soviet submarines with arrays of acoustic sensors moored to the ocean floor.

These various systems were sufficient for the age of massive retaliation. Confirmation of an attack against the U.S. would lead directly to a single presidential order to launch the entire American nuclear arsenal. The Kennedy Administration took the network as it was and began to make a series of incremental improvements in the flexibility and the survivability of U.S. command and control arrangements. The first objective was to insure that a launch order, once given, would reach the intended recipient. The second objective was to prevent the unauthorized release of a nuclear weapon. The final objective was to create a mechanism by which the president could theoretically manage a nuclear campaign.

On February 3, 1961, the Strategic Air Command began around-the-clock operations of an airborne command post, code-named Looking Glass, with a two-star Air Force general in command. The communications equipment onboard was designed to retransmit a presidential launch order directly to the missile sites or individual bombers in the event that SAC headquarters was destroyed by a surprise attack. Steps were taken by McNamara to deploy additional airborne command posts using KC-135 aircraft, and some B-47 bombers were retrofitted to serve as radio relay stations. Construction began on a hardened command post for SAC and an alternate National Command Center located in Maryland. In June 1962 a new National Military Command Center was established to process detailed warning information and issue instructions to U.S. strategic nuclear forces. The Kennedy Administration also requested the same year an appropriation of $23 million for the development of an electronic lock that would permit the arming of a nuclear warhead only by remote control.

The "No-Cities" Doctrine

The Kennedy Administration's actions in the sphere of command and control were matched by a concerted effort to bring a greater degree of discrimination to U.S. targeting plans. During the 1950s, the armed services followed a catch-as-catch-can approach to nuclear targeting, with two or more services sometimes allocating weapons to destroy the same target. In August 1960 Secretary of Defense Thomas Gates established the Joint Strategic Target Planning Staff to centralize the process and end the jurisdictional infighting. The Commander-in-Chief of SAC was designated as the director of this organization, and he was seconded by a Navy admiral. Six months later, JSTPS produced a comprehensive nuclear attack plan that was called the Single Integrated Operations Plan or SIOP I. According to this plan, the United States would fire its entire nuclear arsenal in a single coordinated attack against every major city in Eastern Europe, the Soviet Union and mainland China as well as at a host of military and economic targets. These included railroad marshalling yards, submarine bases, airfields, hydroelectric dams, oil fields, and mines. JSTPS estimated that between 360 and 425 million people would be killed in the attack.[22]

McNamara was briefed at length during his first week at the Pentagon on an alternative to such carnage by William Kaufmann, a senior staff member of the Rand Corporation. Kaufmann and his colleagues had devised a targeting plan called the "No-Cities" doctrine.[23] They argued that it was in the interest of the United States not to strike Soviet cities first. Such restraint was free of risk and of great potential benefit to the survival of the United States in the event of nuclear war.

The rationale was straightforward. If the Soviets abstained from attacking our cities, we would not strike their cities. If either side broke the "rule," his population would suffer the consequences. As long as the "rule" was followed, the Rand proponents were confident that the U.S. could coerce the Soviets into surrender with a series of circumscribed nuclear strikes.

McNamara quickly adopted the strategy as his own. He ordered the Joint Chiefs of Staff to begin to overhaul SIOP I and identify priority targets that did not overlap with Soviet cities, and other targets that could be attacked later in the campaign. Between 1961 and 1962, individual target packages were developed for the Soviet Union, China, and the countries in Eastern Europe. Within each package, the targets were broken out as either urban industrial centers, military targets not located near cities, or military targets regardless of location. A special target package was produced for the city of Moscow on the assumption that there would be no one to negotiate with unless the Soviet leadership was spared.[24]

During the course of his testimony before the House Appropriations Subcommittee in January 1962, McNamara was asked to define the circumstances in which it would be in the interest of the United States to spare Soviet cities in a nuclear exchange. He refused to answer the question directly, although he admitted it was unlikely that the Soviets would spare American cities. McNamara continued to champion the "No-Cities" doctrine despite that fact.[25] McNamara addressed the issue of flexible targeting directly in a speech to the American Bar Association on February 17, 1962:

> We may have to retaliate with a single massive attack. Or, we may be able to use our retaliatory forces to limit damage done to ourselves and our allies by knocking out the enemy bases before he has time to launch his second salvos. We can seek to terminate a war on favorable terms by using our forces as a bargaining weapon — by threatening further attack. In any case, our larger reserve of protected firepower would give an enemy an incentive to avoid our cities and to stop a war. Our new policy gives us the flexibility to choose among several operational plans, but does not require that we make any advance commitment with respect to doctrine or targets.[26]

McNamara carried this message to Athens in May for the annual meeting of the NATO Council of Ministers. His remarks were classified, but according to one knowledgable source, his purpose was to discuss the risks of NATO's over-dependence on nuclear weapons and dissuade France from building an independent nuclear deterrent.

In the process, McNamara gave the ministers the most forthright exposition of U.S. plans for nuclear operations they had ever heard.[27]

On his return to Washington, McNamara decided to incorporate portions of his Athens speech into a commencement address he was invited to give at the University of Michigan on 16 June.[28] President Kennedy was not pleased with the idea. He did not want to rankle President de Gaulle, nor did he want to bait Soviet propagandists. Bundy prevailed upon the president to let McNamara go ahead with the speech with the assurance that he, Bundy, would "...work with Bob's people line by line and word by word."[29]

The speech McNamara gave at Ann Arbor corresponded closely to the draft he sent to Secretary Rusk and McGeorge Bundy. The central theme, of course, was nuclear strategy.

> The U.S. has come to the conclusion that, to the extent feasible, basic military strategy in a possible general nuclear war should be approached in much the same way that more conventional military operations have been regarded in the past. That is to say, the principal military objectives, in the event of a nuclear war stemming from a major attack on the Alliance, would be the destruction of the enemy's military forces, not of his civilian population ... we are giving a possible opponent the strongest imaginable incentive to refrain from striking our own cities.[30]

The discussion of the "No-Cities" doctrine was noticeably less explicit than originally planned, as illustrated by the two following points in McNamara's 31 May draft.

> The nature of the Alliance nuclear forces makes it possible to retain major strategic strength ... holding enemy cities hostage while attacks confined to his military forces are in progress.

> We have also instituted a number of programs which will enable the Alliance to engage in a controlled and flexible nuclear response in the event that deterrence should fail. Whether the Soviet Union will do likewise must remain uncertain. All we can say is that the Kremlin has very strong incentives — in large part provided by the nuclear strength of the Alliance — to adopt similar strategies and programs.[31]

The speech sparked a firestorm of criticism in the media. Some interpreted the speech "as meaning the United States is moving toward acceptance of the inevitability of nuclear war to be conducted under rules laid down in advance." Others equated a counterforce strategy with a first strike posture.[32]

A more thoughtful critique appeared in the *New Republic* by Michael Brower. In Brower's opinion, the "No-Cities" doctrine made sense only if a nation already possessed a well-developed counter-force capability and decisive nuclear superiority. It was equally clear that both the United States and the Soviet Union could not possess this superiority simultaneously. Thus, Brower concluded that the Soviets would be unlikely to adopt a "No-Cities" strategy so long as the U.S.S.R. remained weaker than the United States.[33]

Morton Halperin spoke in favor of the strategy on the pages of the same journal. Halperin expected a future circumstance in which both sides possessed a substantial number of invulnerable forces. Neither the United States nor the Soviet Union, whether striking first or second, could hope to destroy most of its opponent's forces and thereby escape serious damage. Halperin contended that McNamara tried to make the point at Ann Arbor that "it was preferable to hold a large part of our strategic forces in reserve rather than to attack cities simply because there were no other targets to hit." Halperin concluded that the possession of invulnerable forces by both sides could slow the pace of a nuclear war if it happened, in contrast to the widely held view that the outcome of a thermonuclear war would be decided during the first hours of the conflict.[34]

The Soviet response to the controversy was harsh. Marshal V.D. Sokolovskiy accused the United States of attempting to codify "rules" of engagement that made nuclear war more acceptable. "The idea of the so-called *new strategy* . . . is clear — to be the first to strike and then to try to weaken the strength of a counterblow against U.S. territory, to reduce the number of its own losses and to force its will on the enemy."[35]

McNamara refused to bow to his critics and jettison his "No-Cities" strategy. The Defense Department's Posture Statement for FY 1964 included an endorsement of flexible targeting, but McNamara's enthusiasm had cooled considerably. The Secretary of Defense was confident that the United States would retain its strategic superiority for at least the next five years.[36] History proved McNamara wrong; Khrushchev's successors refused to remain militarily inferior to the United States regardless of the economic costs. The Secretary of Defense, however, clearly understood the logic of the strategic competition. McNamara startled the members of the House Appropriations Subcommittee when he announced the "grim prospect" of mutual nuclear deterrence. "More armaments, whether offensive or defensive, cannot solve this dilemma," he declared.

> We have not found it feasible, at this time, to provide a capability
> for insuring the destruction of any very large portion of the fully
> hard ICBM sites, if the Soviets build them in quantity, or of missile
> launching submarines.[37]

The following year, McNamara announced that the U.S. deterrent should be large enough "to ensure the destruction, singularly or
in combination, of the Soviet Union, Communist China and the Communist satellites as national societies, under the worst possible circumstances of war outbreak...."[38] McNamara had come full circle.
His aggressive search for targeting options had led him back to the
strategy he originally challenged: massive retaliation.

Revisionism and Orthodoxy in Soviet Military Thought

The first crack in the facade of Stalinist military dogma occurred
during the fall of 1953. The September issue of *Voennaya Mysl'*,
published by the General Staff, carried an article entitled, "On the
Question of the Laws of Military Science." The author was the journal's own editor, Major General N.A. Talenskiy. Talenskiy maintained that the laws of war applied equally to both sides. In so doing,
he recognized the commonality of danger and opportunity facing the
combatants in a nuclear war. Talenskiy also raised the possibility that
victory might come quickly in a future war through a rapid succession
of nuclear strikes.[39] Criticisms of his work appeared in *Voennaya
Mysl'* in the months that followed. The board of editors closed off the
debate in November 1954 by concluding that the laws of war are ap-
plicable to both sides in a military conflict between antagonistic social
systems. The editors left the issue open to further discussion with the
judgment that "it is not yet possible to propound any final and definite
formulation of the basic law."[40] This point is extremely important
when considering the course of the debate on military science that
preoccupied the Soviet military and political leadership until the late
1960s. By acknowledging the legitimacy of divergent points of view,
the editors of *Voennaya Mysl'* were suggesting that a unified military
doctrine, void of dissent, would be virtually impossible to codify.

The first public admission that a debate was even in progress did
not take place until 1964. The article was entitled, "The Development
of Soviet Military Theory in the Postwar Years," by Colonel I.
Korotkov, and it appeared in the April edition of the *Voenno-
Istoricheskiy Zhurnal*. Korotkov divided the postwar years into two

periods: the first from 1945 to 1954, the second from 1954 until the publication of his article in 1964. He subdivided the latter stage into two distinct phases, 1954 to 1956 and 1956 to 1964.

Korotkov's observations about the first period were predictable. Soviet military theory was "influenced negatively by the cult of personality." Military research relied solely on Soviet combat experience with large-scale operations. According to Korotkov, however, only "successful" Soviet operations were studied; the failures were largely ignored. As a consequence, "military scientific cadres forgot how to think critically." For example, "the significance of surprise was viewed as it had been in 1942 in spite of the fact that the development of atomic weapons pointed out a sharp increase in the role played by surprise from a strategic aspect."[41]

The first stage of the second period (1954–1956) was characterized as a time of "gradual changes." These changes were explained by the incorporation of ballistic missiles and nuclear weapons into the Soviet armed forces. However, "the use of nuclear weapons was still considered within the framework of former methods of waging war and conducting operations." The reasons for this, according to Korotkov, had to do in part with the limited number of nuclear weapons available and the fact that the sole delivery system was aircraft, and that the "combat properties" of these weapons had not been sufficiently studied. More importantly, "new ideas and views were born and solidified in the struggle against old views, making headway with difficulty."[42] This stage closed appropriately enough with the opening of the Twentieth Party Congress in February 1956. Stalin's dethronement signaled the burial of the dogma of "permanently operating factors."

The final stage began with the appearance of the Soviet intercontinental ballistic missile. This required, according to Korotkov, "a radical revision of views on the nature of a possible war, the forms and methods of armed combat, the role and significance of each branch of the armed forces and branches within each branch."[43] These issues stand at the center of Soviet military science and were the subject of intense discussion. The opinion was expressed as early as 1956 that "the most modern weapons would not minimize the *decisive* significance of land armies, the Navy and Air Force, and consequently missiles and nuclear weapons were not recognized as the primary and decisive means of waging war." These theorists admitted, however, that a future war would likely be nuclear. Nevertheless, they insisted that victory was "possible only through a series of major military efforts, each of which would require a rather long period of time." Korotkov attributed these opinions to "the fact that we and our probable opponents at that time did not have a sufficient number of long-range missiles."[44] The emergence of ballistic missiles sparked the appearance of an antithetical point of view. These missile advocates contended that modern technology had now created the conditions for "a swift war of brief duration."[45] In the opinion of one scholar, this dichotomy could be best described as a divergence between *modernists* and *traditionalists* in the Soviet military.[46] Khrushchev was clearly a proponent of the modernist perspective.

The direction of Khrushchev's military thinking became evident shortly after the conclusion of the Twentieth Party Congress in February 1956. At the Congress, Khrushchev declared war was no longer a "fatalistic inevitability." The reason was that the Soviet Union now possessed "formidable means to prevent the imperialists from unleashing war." If they tried, Khrushchev promised them a "smashing rebuff."[47] The source of Khrushchev's confidence was the development of ballistic missiles. In April of 1956, Khrushchev and Bulganin traveled to Great Britain on a good will visit aboard the Soviet battle cruiser *Ordzhonikidze*. Khrushchev noted the admiration of the cruiser by British naval officers at a reception hosted by the First Lord of the Admiralty. With his typical pugnacity, Khrushchev declared that the U.S.S.R. would gladly sell the cruiser to the British because it was obsolete. In his words:

> Besides, cruisers like ours no longer play a decisive role. Nor do bombers. Now it is submarines that rule the sea, and missiles that rule the air — missiles that can strike their targets from great distances.[48]

The Soviet military leaders, however, continued to take the position that the nuclear bomb was not an absolute weapon. In an article published in *Pravda* in August 1956, Marshal Zhukov wrote that "air power and nuclear weapons by themselves cannot determine the outcome of an armed conflict."[49]

In May 1957 a conference was convened to reexamine Soviet military science and scientific research within the armed forces. The following year a seminar began in the Soviet General Staff on problems of future war and the state of Soviet military art. The military theoreticians agreed that Soviet military doctrine must be revised. This would require, however, the explicit participation of the political leadership.

There is little doubt where Khrushchev stood. At a reception in honor of the Forty-Second Anniversary of the Bolshevik Revolution in November 1959, Khrushchev remarked that he did not trust the opinion of his generals, an admission that perhaps the same was true in reverse.[50] Two months later, he tossed the hint at a New Year's reception that he might dismantle the Soviet Army altogether and rely solely on rockets.[51] A fortnight later, Khrushchev announced a fundamental revision of Soviet military doctrine as well as a significant cut in the size of the Soviet Armed Forces in a report to the Fourth Session of the Supreme Soviet. Military manpower was reduced from 3,623,000 to 2,423,000 men.[52] The report was apparently drafted after a consideration of these issues by the Central Committee in December 1959.[53] Marshal M.I. Nedelin was appointed the first Commander-in-Chief of the Strategic Rocket Forces that same month.[54] However, the first public announcement of the organization's existence did not take place until the following June.[55]

Khrushchev justified his proposed reduction on the decisive value of ballistic missiles and nuclear weapons. In the future, he declared, "war would start for the most part deep within the belligerent countries, and not one capital, not one major industrial or administrative center, not one strategic area would escape attack in the first minutes, let alone the first days of the war...."[56] Khrushchev assured those who doubted the wisdom of the reduction that a "comprehensive and detailed study" had been conducted, indicating that Soviet defenses would remain adequate. He announced that manned bombers had "lost their former importance," and that Soviet long-range bomber production had been virtually halted. While surface naval vessels were declared obsolete, Khrushchev stated that submarines were "assuming greater importance." Although the Soviet Union would suffer heavy damage in a nuclear war, he proclaimed that the West would suffer incomparably more. "If the aggressors should start a war," Khrushchev thundered, "it would not only be their last war, but the ruin of capitalism."[57] The most important facet of Khrushchev's speech was also the least noticed in the West: Khrushchev acknowledged the existence of mutual nuclear deterrence.

> But the question suggests itself: Once the possibility is not excluded that some capitalist states are drawing abreast of us in the field of modern armaments, could they not perfidiously attack us first, in order to take advantage of the factor of a surprise attack by such terrible weapons as atomic rockets and thereby gain an advantage for ensuring victory?
>
> No. The present-day means of warfare do not give such advantages to any side. It is impossible to attack first; it doesn't require much brains to do this.[58]

Khrushchev admitted that the troop reductions "represent a powerful reinforcement for fulfilling and over-fulfilling our economic plans." The reason was simply that "a further reduction of the Armed Forces, ... when implemented, will mean that a large number of their military comrades will return to work at enterprises, construction projects, collective and state farms, and scientific and educational institutions."[59]

Khrushchev closed his speech with the announcement that the regime was "studying the question of shifting at some time in the future to the organization of the Armed Forces on a territorial basis."[60] It was unclear whether this proposal was meant to encompass all Soviet forces or was directed towards the formation of a small regular army supplemented by a territorial militia similar to the one that existed during the last two years of Lenin's life. The latter option was the most likely possibility, according to Marshal Malinovskiy.[61] The proposal had some obvious advantages for Khrushchev. By the late 1950s, the substantial decrease in the Soviet birth rate, caused by the Second World War and the food shortages in its immediate aftermath, was having a debilitating effect on the Soviet economy. In 1959 the Soviet Union had 6,915,000 males in the eighteen- to twenty-one-year-old age bracket. By 1964 the figure had dropped to 3,164,000 males, less than one half of the 1959 figure.[62] The reduction would not only ease the labor shortage for the U.S.S.R., but provide a response to ideological pressures from Communist China and bolster Khrushchev's diplomatic and propaganda campaign for disarmament.[63]

The proposal was potentially disastrous from the perspective of a majority of the Soviet officer corps. If implemented, a territorial militia would encourage localism, relegate the military to corvee, and serve as a lever for further cuts in the armed forces.[64] The retirements of Marshals Konev and Sokolovskiy for "health" reasons during the spring of 1960 were the most graphic expression of unrest in the ranks.[65]

Penkovskiy and the "Special Collection"

The Soviet General Staff authorized the periodic publication of a top secret edition of *Voennaya Mysl'* entitled the "Special Collection of Articles" in January 1960, the same month that Khrushchev sounded the death knell of Soviet conventional forces. Our knowledge of the 1958 General Staff Seminars and the "Special Collection" relies totally on a single book, *The Penkovskiy Papers*, that appeared in

1965. The *Papers* are purported to be based on the notes and sketches of Colonel Oleg V. Penkovskiy, a staff officer in the Main Intelligence Directorate (GRU) of the Soviet General Staff who for sixteen months, between April 1961 and August 1962, served as an intelligence agent for the United States and Great Britain. Penkovskiy was arrested in October 1962 along with Greville Wynne, a British businessman, who acted as "cutout" or middleman between Penkovskiy and his Western case officers. On May 11, 1963, after a hastily conducted four-day trial, Penkovskiy was sentenced to death for espionage by the Soviet Supreme Court in Moscow, and Wynne received an eight-year term in prison.

The *Papers* reveal that Penkovskiy provided a copy of the "Special Collection" to CIA and MI-6. Her Majesty's Government has never confirmed nor denied its involvement in the Penkovskiy affair. In 1972, however, the United States did acknowledge the existence of the collection:

> The "Special Collection" contains material of the highest classification, much of which is still extraordinarily relevant to current [Soviet] strategic doctrine and war plans.[66]

Since it is highly unlikely that this material will ever be released, it is impossible to determine with certainty the accuracy of the extracts from the "Special Collection" contained in the *Penkovskiy Papers*. The basic question, then, is whether the *Papers* are the authentic voice of Oleg Penkovskiy or a contrivance by the Americans and British.

In a commentary on the book prepared for the *Saturday Review*, Harry Schwartz complained that "the material in this volume that can be checked is the sort of thing that could have been written by a Soviet defector living in the West or even by an American or Britain familiar with what the West knows about the Soviet system."[67] Peter Deriabin, the acknowledged recipient of the *Papers*, and their translator, was a former Soviet intelligence officer before his defection.

Walter Laquer, on the other hand, speculated that the book's anecdotal style might indicate that the book was an edited version of taped interviews that took place with American and British intelligence officers in London. "It is just possible," he wrote, "that some bits and pieces were added from the actual intelligence reports sent by Penkovskiy from Moscow."[68] Thomas Wolfe found "no convincing internal evidence that the account as a whole is a synthetic contrivance."[69]

Bearing in mind Wolfe's counsel that the *Papers* should be used with "caution and discrimination," Penkovskiy's comments on the "Special Collection" are as follows: All of the authors recognized the importance of the first nuclear strike. Strategic nuclear missiles were expected to play a "tremendous role" in the initial period of war and make it possible "to achieve the necessary strategic goals of the war within the shortest possible time."[70] Some of the authors, however, suggested that the following qualification should be included as a part of Soviet military doctrine: "Try to achieve victory with a short war (by a lightning strike) but be prepared for a prolonged war."[71]

The *Penkovskiy Papers* identify only two of the articles in the collection: the first, by Lieutenant General A.I. Gastilovich, entitled "The Theory of Military Art Needs Review," and the second, an untitled article by Major General M. Goryainov.[72] Gastilovich, a firm advocate of missiles, criticized those who attempted "to fit missile-nuclear weapons into the framework of the familiar needs of our military doctrine.... We forget," Gastilovich argued, "that this doctrine bases itself on the use of weapons not comparable with contemporary weapons." Goryainov follows a similar tack and states that "we [the Soviet Union] must go faster and further both in the theory of using nuclear/missile weapons and in their production." His reason is that *"Victory by one side depends on readiness and ability to finish the war in the shortest period of time."*[73]

The basic issues considered in the "Special Collection" were also discussed in the Soviet military press, although less categorically. Malinovskiy, in a speech to the Chelyabinsk election district following Khrushchev's troop reduction announcement, used the same example as Gastilovich.

> It appears that approximately 100 of these nuclear charges exploded in a brief space of time over a state with a highly developed industry and an area of about 300,000 to 500,000 square kilometers would be enough to turn all its industrial areas and centers of political administration into a heap of ruins and the territory into a lifeless desert contaminated with lethal radioactive substances.[74]

Furthermore, he tempered Khrushchev's statement on troop reductions:

> Our missile units are undoubtedly the principal aspect of our armed forces, but we realize that not all the tasks of war can be accomplished by one type of troops. For this reason, assuming that military operations can be conducted successfully in a modern war only by the coordinated use of all armaments, we are leaving all the

aspects of our armed forces at a definite numerical strength, each in its rational proportions.[75]

Khrushchev's views were supported by the military's principal iconoclast, Major General Talenskiy. Talenskiy presented his views in the October 1960 issue of *International Affairs*. He stated that "the basic economic and political centers" would be the primary targets of nuclear strikes in a future war. Talenskiy relegated conventional operations, as did Khrushchev, to an ancillary role.[76] Colonel A.M. Iovlev took exception to this interpretation of ground operations six months later on the pages of *Krasnaya Zvezda*. Iovlev conceded that rocket troops were the "foundation" of Soviet military power, but he asserted that the "complete rout of the enemy can be achieved only by the combined efforts of all types of armed forces and service branches."[77]

In Search of a Consensus

The Berlin crisis surely impressed upon the Soviets the need to establish some semblance of accommodation between their competing schools of military thought. The first step was taken by Marshal Malinovskiy during his address to the Twenty-Second Party Congress on October 23, 1961. Soviet military doctrine, he declared, is predicated upon the following assumptions: Any future world war will "inescapably assume the character of a nuclear rocket war." The primary objective of the Soviet armed forces is "to repulse reliably a surprise attack of the enemy" since these strikes will probably determine the subsequent course of the conflict. These preemptive strikes would be made against the enemy's armed forces, his industrial centers and communications junctions, and "everything which feeds the war." The war will be fought by mass armies, and "the final victory . . . can only be achieved as a result of the joint actions of all types of armed forces."[78]

The following month, Malinovskiy turned his attention to the specific issue of how to fight and win a nuclear war. Malinovskiy told the readers of *Krasnaya Zvezda* that "the main general task of all our armed forces has been and is to study and work out the methods of combat organization of troops under conditions of the utilization of nuclear rocket weapons, the methods for reliably warding off a sudden nuclear attack of the aggressor and for thwarting his aggressive intentions by an opportune crushing blow."[79]

The indoctrination process began in earnest on April 4, 1962, when *Krasnaya Zvezda* published a question submitted to the editorial staff:

> At the Twenty-Second Party Congress N.S. Khrushchev said: "Success in socialist production and in Soviet science and engineering has allowed us to bring about the present revolution in military affairs." What does this mean?

This primitive question from the obscure Lieutenant Martynov became the pretext for a massive propaganda campaign to instruct all ranks of the Soviet armed forces about the changes in military doctrine.[80] The appearance of *Voennaya Strategiya* was the premier event of this campaign.

Sokolovskiy's Volume and Its Critics

In August 1962, a few months before the outbreak of the Cuban missile crisis, a book appeared in Moscow entitled *Voennaya Strategia*. The book was prepared by a group of eleven authors under the editorial supervision of a former Chief of the Soviet General Staff, Marshal V.D. Sokolovskiy. Sokolovskiy acknowledged, in his editorial introduction, that the present volume was the first comprehensive treatment of military strategy since the publication of *Strategia* in 1926 by A. Svechin, a leading military theorist of the 1920s and the first Chief of the General Staff. In an apparent allusion to the "Special Collection," Sokolovskiy stated that this book was written because of the "obvious dearth in the open literature of works that give a general understanding of military strategy in all its facets."[81]

Voennaya Strategia is about the means of waging and, if possible, winning a nuclear war.

> In modern warfare, military strategy has become the strategy of missile and nuclear strikes in depth along with the simultaneous use of all branches of the armed forces in order to achieve complete defeat of the enemy and the destruction of his economic potential and armed forces throughout his entire territory; such war aims are to be accomplished within a short period of time.[82]

The main goals of the war would be achieved by the Strategic Rocket Forces (SRF). Air and ground forces would operate in tandem to destroy enemy units in the continental theaters of military operations, occupy enemy territory and prevent the enemy from invading Soviet territory and the territory of its allies in Eastern Europe. The air defense forces would defend the country from nuclear strikes, and the navy would engage hostile forces at sea, open sea lines of communications and defend costal areas.[83] To achieve final victory, the Soviet armed forces must "smash the enemy's armed forces completely, to deprive him of strategic areas of deployment, liquidate his military bases, and occupy his strategically important regions."[84] Therefore, "the main task in Soviet military strategy is . . . the working out of the means for reliably repelling a surprise nuclear attack by an aggressor."[85] The primary targets for the SRF's missile strikes would be the enemy's strategic weapons, his military and economic potential, the government and military control systems and his troop units."[86]

The first edition of *Voennaya Strategia* did contain several ambiguous passages. The book drew attention to the need to prepare for local wars:

> Offense and defense, as forms of strategic operations, can retain their significance in military operations of conventional forces in certain types of local wars, the probability of which cannot be excluded even under contemporary conditions.[87]

This assertion was balanced by the familiar Soviet bromide that "an armed conflict will inevitably develop into an all-out war, if nuclear powers are drawn into it."[88] Contingent explanations were also given on the size of the armed forces and the possible duration of the initial period of war.

The Sokolovskiy volume was not without its critics in the Soviet Union. The majority of reviews emphasized the authors' sins of omission rather than commission. Admiral Alafuzov complained that the book "inadequately" covered the principles of naval strategy. "In discussing massed rocket strikes," Alafuzov wrote, "the authors failed to mention rocket-carrying nuclear submarines which are in fact mobile rocket launchers having the capability of occupying positions to launch rockets quickly and covertly and then departing quickly, thus avoiding enemy retaliation."[89] General Kurochkin believed that the authors had not "assigned sufficient weight to, nor analyzed deeply enough the role and methods of operations of the ground forces."[90] Finally, *Voennaya Strategia* was taken to task by A. Golubev for displaying an "insufficiently attentive attitude" towards military history.[91] Far more serious charges were presented in an article written by the editor of *Voyennyy Vestnik*, Colonel V. Zemskov, and his co-author, Colonel A. Yakimovskiy. In their opinion, "the economic, political and morale factors in the preparation of the country for war belong to the realm of politics and not strategy." In other words, the responsibility for these measures rested with the Communist Party and the Soviet Government, not with the military.[92]

These comments were indicative of a rather thinly veiled dispute underway in 1961 and 1962 regarding the role and responsibility of the professional military in the formulation of Soviet security policy. Malinovskiy failed to mention any personal contribution by Khrushchev to the development of Soviet military doctrine in his address to the Twenty-Second Party Congress in October 1961. The first edition of *Voennaya Strategia* was equally blatant in its disregard of Party prerogatives. "Military doctrine is not thought out or compiled by a single person or group of persons; it comes out of the vital activities of the state as a whole, and it is the result of a quite complex and lengthy historical process of the creation and development of official ideas."[93]

Khrushchev and the Party began to reassert their authority in military matters in the aftermath of the Cuban missile crisis. The vehicle was a pamphlet written by Marshal Malinovskiy entitled *Bditel'no Stoyat Ha Strazhe Mira*. Signed to press on November 28, 1962, the pamphlet was not released to the public until April 1963. The purpose of this monograph was to assert the complete dominance of the Party in general, and Nikita Khrushchev in particular, in military affairs and in the codification of military doctrine. Malinovskiy now declared that "Military doctrine is developed and determined by the political leadership of the State." Moreover, he gave pride of place to Khrushchev's January 1960 speech to the Supreme Soviet and described that speech as the "first detailed statement of the principles of contemporary Soviet military doctrine."[94]

On May 23, 1963, the Ministry of Defense sponsored a conference on the question of "The Essence and Content of Soviet Military Doctrine," the title of a report written by Major General A.A. Prokhorov. The purpose of the conference was to eradicate any remaining definitional difficulties surrounding the proper interpretation of Soviet military doctrine.[95] A brochure entitled *Sovetskaya Voennaya Doctrina* was signed to press the same month. The author, Colonel-General N.A. Lomov, was effusive in his praise of Khrushchev and the role of the Party in military affairs.

> The fundamentals of military doctrine are determined by the political leadership of the country, since only it has the jurisdiction and competence to solve problems of building military power...[96]

The new stress on Party prerogatives was equally evident in the second edition of *Voennaya Strategia* published in August 1963. Marshal Sokolovskiy refused, however, to accept the criticism of Zemskov and Yakimovskiy. "The investigation," he wrote, "of the problems of leadership in the preparation of the country to repel aggression, as well as the problems of the leadership of the armed forces, should also enter into the mission of Soviet military doctrine."[97]

Voennaya Strategia also created intense interest in the United States among scholars and government officials alike. Two translations of the book, including analytic commentaries, were published, and the book quickly received extensive media attention. A range of interpretations about the significance of *Voennaya Strategia* was exhibited at a conference held in the Spring of 1963 by the Georgetown Center for Strategic Studies. British historian and strategist B.H. Liddell-Hart claimed derisively that *Military Strategy* was "palpably inadequate to overcome Soviet deficiencies in strategic thinking." In rebuttal, Stefan Possony called attention to the danger of dismissing Soviet military thought as "extraordinarily backward." "It is imprudent for our side," he warned, "to assume that we are more intelligent in strategic matters than the other side."[98]

Virtually all of the participants agreed that the book was part of the internal military debate in the Soviet Union. Hanson Baldwin of the *New York Times* observed that the book "plainly reflects the continued conflict between the ground marshals . . . and the new missile experts." Thomas Wolfe and Raymond Garthoff considered the book to be additional evidence of civil-military tensions in the Soviet Union. Wolfe saw the book as "primarily a document from the military side of the house that strikes a balance in the debate." Garthoff, on the other hand, asserted that the book was indicative of "indirect lobbying" by the military to get its views accepted by the political leadership.[99]

Robert McNamara was unimpressed with *Military Strategy*. Nowhere in the book did he find "a sophisticated analysis of nuclear war." In McNamara's considered opinion, the authors "never really had exposed to them the destructive power of nuclear weapons."[100]

Commonalities and Differences

Robert McNamara and Rodion Malinovskiy typified the mainstream of strategic thought in their respective countries; McNamara was the technocratic manager preoccupied with the problems of force levels, and Malinovskiy, the hardened combat veteran concerned just as much with the realities of battlefield. The obvious difference between the civilian manager and the military commander can be overdone. Each stood at the pinnacle of his military establishments. As a consequence, they shared a series of common concerns, if not a common perspective.

The first issue was simply the problem of asserting executive leadership in a competitive bureaucratic environment and fashioning a unified defense policy in the face of inter-service hostility. McNamara enforced unity by the strength of his own personality, the complete support of the White House, and his absolute control of the preparation of the defense budget. The Planning-Programming-Budgetary System severely limited the ability of the armed services to cut a deal amongst themselves and present the Pentagon's civilian leadership with a budgetary *fait accompli*. McNamara recruited a group of young economists and scientists to make the system work. The "whiz kids," as they were called by their detractors, were often brilliant in their efforts to make the Defense Department a more efficient and productive organization. Their conceit, however, inevitably rankled the admirals and generals of the uniformed services. The Commander of SAC, General Thomas S. Powers, probably expressed best the sense of outrage among many military officers in McNamara's Pentagon. Powers had no doubt about his mission: "The task of the military in war [is] to kill human beings and destroy man-made objects." This truth seemed to be lost, in his opinion, on the civilian "computer types" making defense policy "who don't know their ass from a hole in the ground."[101] There may have been more than a grain of truth in the general's outburst. McNamara and his aides devoted considerable attention to the short-lived but much-discussed "No-Cities" doctrine. Their strategy of flexible response required extraordinary restraint, the careful selection of targets, and an almost compulsive search for options. The entire edifice would have probably crumbled in the event of war. As one senior official in the Pentagon put it, "You can't crank anger into a calculating machine."[102]

The published record still provides only brief glimpses of the bureaucratic strife Malinovskiy faced. In principle, the conflict between the U.S. Air Force and Navy over nuclear strategy was no different from the infighting that took place in the Soviet military establishment between the proponents of the Strategic Rocket Forces and the generals of the Soviet Ground Forces. How Malinovskiy managed to strike a balance between both constituencies is still uncertain. He initially supported Khrushchev's efforts to slash military manpower and rely primarily upon nuclear weapons. At the Twenty-Second Party Congress, however, he seized the middle ground of the debate and announced that massive armies were just as important to victory in a future war as ballistic missiles. Malinovskiy's speech was certainly at odds with Khrushchev's own policy preference, but Malinovskiy carefully avoided an open rupture with the political leadership.

Malinovskiy and McNamara shared a second concern: what to do if nuclear deterrence failed. In this respect, both men were prisoners of ignorance. The structure of Soviet military thought, with its precise definitions of military doctrine and military strategy, seems to suggest a more rigorous and serious approach to national security than exists among American defense intellectuals. Malinovskiy, however, had no better idea of how to wage and win a nuclear war than his American counterpart. McNamara finessed the dilemma by propounding the dictum of assured destruction, which was not a strategy but a formula for national suicide. The destruction of an opponent's population centers, in the event of nuclear war, was no less important to Khrushchev and his marshals. The difference, however, was their willingness to press for some protection of the Soviet population no matter how marginal the prospects for suvival. "If the enemy starts a war," Khrushchev observed, "then it is your duty to do everything possible to survive the war and to achieve victory in the end."[103]

Chapter 3

The Preconditions for Deterrence

Diplomacy without arms is music without an instrument.
Frederick the Great

Sputnik and the "Missile Gap"

On August 26, 1957, the Soviet news agency TASS announced the successful test flight of the world's first intercontinental ballistic missile, the SS-6. The announcement did not fail to point out the obvious military implications of the event. The test demonstrated "that it is possible to direct rockets to any part of the world."[1] Six weeks later, on 4 October, the Soviets used an SS-6 booster to launch the first artificial satellite, Sputnik I.

Prior to both triumphs, the Soviets had little choice but to respond to the American lead in strategic nuclear weapons. President Eisenhower announced in January 1954 that the future security of the United States would depend on the "creation, maintenance, and full exploitation of modern air power."[2] In May the Soviet Air Defense Forces were redesignated as a separate service. That same year, the Politburo decided to forego construction of a large surface navy and strive to increase Soviet air and missile power. Khrushchev justified the decision to Admiral N.G. Kuznetsov in this way:

> Let's put off indefinitely the question of building up our navy and concentrate instead on the development of our air force and missiles. Any future war will be won in the air, not on the sea; and our potential adversaries are equipped to attack us from the air. Therefore, we should think first about improving our air defenses and our means of counterattack.[3]

By 1955 the U.S. had deployed around the Eurasian periphery more than 500 aircraft and cruise missiles (Mace and Matador) capable of nuclear strikes against the Soviet homeland. These forces included B-47 medium-range bombers at forward bases and fighter-bombers on land and aboard aircraft carriers. The Soviets, in turn, improved their early warning capabilities, deployed significant numbers of surface-to-air missiles, and introduced high-speed interceptor aircraft capable of all-weather operations.

The Soviets began to deploy their new medium- and long-range bombers between 1954 and 1955. The Soviet Air Force had 1,000 Tu-16 Badgers, and over 100 Tu-20 Bears and 30 Mya-4 Bisons by 1959. However, the Badger lacked the range to cover a significant number of U.S. targets, the Bear had the range but was very slow, and the Bison was never produced in large enough numbers to present a significant threat. At the same time, the Soviets constructed an extensive system of forward air bases in the Arctic, but these were more than offset by the U.S. bases ringing the Soviet Union. Khrushchev admitted in his memoirs that the "range requirements set by our planners for a strategic bomber were beyond the reach of our technological capability." The U.S. could dispatch aircraft from European bases, but "we had no way of stationing our planes on the edge of the American border."[4]

The advent of the ballistic missile solved Mr. Khrushchev's strategic dilemma. In an interview with James Reston, three days after the launch of Sputnik I, Khrushchev declared that the Soviet Union now possessed "all the rockets we need: long-range rockets, intermediate rockets, and close-range rockets." "Of course," he added, "these are not the limits of what can be achieved, for engineering is not marking time, but these means fully insure our defenses."[5] During an interview in November, the *New York Times'* Moscow correspondent, Harry Schwartz, asked Khrushchev if he believed "that the Soviet Union has surpassed the United States not only regarding the intercontinental ballistic missile, but also in the manufacture of rockets in general." The Soviet premier's response: "Most assuredly."[6] Neither reporter realized that he had been deceived.

The SS-6 was a flawed giant and vulnerable to attack. The unique first stage configuration of the SS-6 (one main engine with a cluster of four large strap-on engines) could not be emplaced in a protective silo. Several hours were required to prepare the SS-6 for launch because its volatile propellant could not be stored onboard. In addition, the rocket was guided by radio command and needed frequent mid-course corrections by tracking stations. The SS-6, therefore, presented the Soviet leadership with a problem. To admit these shortcomings would be unthinkable from the standpoint of secrecy alone. Besides,

Khrushchev was about to open his campaign to overtake the United States economically and to resolve the German question in favor of the Soviet Union.

Khrushchev and his colleagues used the afterglow of Sputnik to alter their weapon priorities and emphasize the procurement of theater nuclear systems. At about the same time, the Soviets decided to limit drastically the production of long-range bombers.[7] Deployment of the 1,000 nm SS-4 began in late 1958 and 200 missiles were in place by 1960. The Soviet Union's first generation of sea-launched ballistic missiles, the SS-N-4, entered service in 1958 on six medium-range, diesel-powered Victor and Zulu class patrol submarines converted to carry two missile launchers in their conning towers. These missiles had a range of 350 nm and they could only be fired when the submarine was on the surface. The Soviet Union's first nuclear submarine, the Hotel-I class, appeared in 1959 with three SS-N-4 missiles aboard. The Soviet leadership seemed willing to defer any large-scale ICBM deployment until the production of their third-generation missiles, the SS-9 and SS-11. Both missiles were under development in 1958.

The tenor of Khrushchev's initial interviews after the Soviet space successes suggests that the decision to mislead the West about the true state of Soviet military capabilities predated these events. Two years earlier, at the July Aviation Day celebrations in Moscow, the Soviets flew the same squadron of Bear bombers in large circles, reappearing every few minutes, to persuade the diplomats and military attaches present that the Soviets were committed to increasing their long-range bomber force.[8]

Khrushchev's missile diplomacy was aimed at concealing the modest scope of the Soviet ICBM program, and creating an atmosphere of mistrust between the United States and its European allies.[9] Germany, Britain, and Italy became the targets of Khrushchev's most blatant threats. In November 1958, he announced that "production of ICBMs has been successfully set up."[10] Six months later, Khrushchev warned a group of West German newspaper editors that "the Western Powers would be literally wiped off the face of the earth" in the event of war. He told Averell Harriman in May that if NATO began a war over Berlin, "we may die, but the rockets will fly automatically."[11] In July the Soviet premier treated his guest, Richard Nixon, to a joke that he understood to be current in England about pessimists and optimists. The pessimists said only six atomic bombs would be needed to wipe out Great Britain, while the optimists said nine or ten would be required.[12] Khrushchev's campaign reached its crescendo in January 1960, when he claimed that the U.S. was five years behind the Soviet Union in the development of rocket technology.[13]

Khrushchev's spate of remarks fueled a crisis of confidence in the United States and Western Europe. The Eisenhower Administration hastened to mollify European fears by pledging deployment of American MRBMs in Europe. Sixty Thor missiles became operational in Britain in 1959. Expenditures on strategic missiles rose from less than $160 million in 1955 to $3.3 billion in 1960.[14] Most of these funds were directed towards the Polaris and Minuteman programs. Public concern, however, was not limited to defense preparedness. Serious questions were raised about the future ability of the United States to compete in science and technology with the Soviet Union. The administration and Congress responded with such measures as the National Defense Education Act.

John Kennedy did not enter the fray until the following summer. His views were directly influenced by Lieutenant General James Gavin, whose ideas appeared in a book called *War and Peace in the Space Age*, and by syndicated columnist Joseph Alsop. Gavin defined the "missile gap," which was to appear between 1960 and 1964, as a period "in which our own offensive and defensive missile capabilities will lag so far behind those of the Soviets as to place us in a position of great peril."[15] Alsop served as a conduit for Air Force–inspired leaks of information from National Intelligence Estimates that indicated a growth in the Soviet ability to conduct a first-strike attack against the United States. In a column published by the *Washington Post* on 18 August, Alsop predicted that the Soviet Union was expected to deploy 500 ICBMs by 1960, an additional 500 the following year, and achieve an operational inventory of 2,000 ICBMs by the end of 1963. In comparison, the United States would field only a force of 130 ICBMs and a few Polaris submarines.[16]

A debate erupted on the floor of the Senate two weeks later following a report published in the *St. Louis Post-Dispatch* that the Rand Corporation was engaged in a "study of the circumstances in which the United States ought to surrender" as part of its examination of the implications of the missile gap. Angered, Senator Richard Russell of Georgia promptly introduced an amendment to a military appropriations bill to forbid the Defense Department to spend any of its funds "on plans for the surrender of the United States." Later in the day, Kennedy delivered his speech on the "missile gap."[17]

Kennedy began his speech with an excerpt from English history. The loss of Calais in 1558 forced the English to reexamine their national interests and sparked the development of a maritime strategy.

Kennedy asserted that the United States was about to lose its own Calais — strategic superiority. Therefore, the United States must consider an equally dramatic change in strategy. The prospect of imminent strategic inferiority obliged the United States to make "the most of the enemy's weaknesses — and thus to buy the time and opportunity necessary to regain the upper hand."[18]

Kennedy argued that a ratio of military power favorable to the Soviet Union might happen so dramatically "during the years of the gap, as to open to them a new shortcut to world domination." In the years of the gap, he explained, the Soviets could be expected to use their superior striking power in ballistic missiles to achieve their objectives by intimidation. Soviet missile power would serve as "a shield from behind which they will slowly, but surely, advance — through Sputnik diplomacy, limited brush-fire wars, indirect aggression, intimidation and subversion, internal revolution, increased prestige or influence, and the vicious blackmail of our allies," as the balance of power gradually shifted against the United States. Each of these probes would weaken the West, "but none will seem sufficiently significant by itself to justify our initiating a nuclear war which might destroy us."[19] Kennedy now joined other congressional Democrats who demanded immediate increases in defense spending and a radical revision of American grand strategy. The "missile gap" became the vehicle for these demands during the 1960 presidential campaign. Kennedy readily wielded this club during the campaign despite his awareness that the "missile gap" was a myth.

The senator was briefed during the summer of 1960 at his home in Hyannis, Massachusetts, by a Naval Intelligence officer, who cautioned him that the latest National Intelligence Estimates did not support the frightening calculations of Soviet missile strength rampant in the press.[20] He was also briefed in September at his Senate office by the Director of the Joint Staff, General Earle Wheeler. Kennedy closed the discussion by asking Wheeler, "General, don't you have any doubting Thomases in the Pentagon?"[21] Kennedy claimed as late as the middle of October that the United States was "moving into a period when the Soviet Union will be outproducing us two to three to one in the field of missiles — a period relatively vulnerable when our retaliatory force will be in danger of destruction through a Soviet surprise attack."[22]

Ambition was clearly one important reason for Kennedy's distortion of the strategic equation. In Henry Trewitt's words, Kennedy, after all, was "a politician just short of the greatest prize the nation could offer."[23] There was, however, an important strategic dimension to Kennedy's use of the "missile gap." Military superiority was central to his world view. In a speech at the Coliseum in Raleigh, North Carolina, Kennedy affirmed that the security of the United States demanded nothing less than absolute military superiority over the Soviet Union and China.

> We want an America which has a military strength second to none — strength sufficient to convince an enemy that an attack would bring disaster. To do this we need two things: an invulnerable atomic striking force which can survive an enemy attack and still remain in possession of its ability to retaliate, and a modern conventional force to intervene quickly and effectively to halt communist aggression in any quarter of the globe.[24]

Action and Reaction on the "Missile Gap"

When the Kennedy Administration took office in January 1961, the Soviets had no operational ICBMs except for a handful of missiles at the Tyuratam and Kapustin Yar test facilities. Construction of an SS-6 ICBM base at Plesetsk near Archangel in northwest Russia began in early 1960, but it was not completed until 1961 and only four SS-6 launch pads were actually installed.[25] Nevertheless, the Kennedy Administration added nearly $6 billion to the Eisenhower Administration's budgetary estimate for FY 1962 of $41.9 billion. About one-third of this increase was devoted to a significant procurement of silo-based Minuteman missiles and Polaris submarines. By the end of 1964, the United States had deployed 931 ICBMs and 320 SLBMs. Three years later, the inventory of strategic ballistic missiles reached the ceiling of 1,710 imposed by Mr. McNamara more than four years earlier. However, the Soviet Union was now in the midst of its own ballistic missile buildup. The Soviet ICBM force approached numerical parity with the United States within two years. By the end of December 1970, the Soviet Union had deployed more than 1,400 ICBMs, including 970 silo-based SS-9 and SS-11 missiles, and 100 additional launchers were under construction.

Conventional interpretations of the Soviet ballistic missile build-up typically emphasize the influence of the Cuban missile crisis on the revitalization of Soviet military power. Actually, Brezhnev and Kosygin probably reconfirmed Khrushchev's missile decisions and simply accelerated the rate of deployment. It seems likely that the Soviets laid the foundation for their missile program in the 1960s by substantially expanding military research and development expenditures from 1954 to 1958 when actual procurement remained constant or even declined. The Seven Year Plan that began in 1959 provided additional increases in Soviet defense spending.[26] Few scholars, however, would disagree with Thomas Wolfe's assessment:

> Cuba certainly was important as a catalyst of Soviet resolve to catch up strategically, and it helped to create the "never again" syndrome exhibited by various Soviet leaders. But it did not start the process of competition, nor — for that matter — did it really set the terms of the competition in the sixties. What had more effect on the size and composition of the Soviet strategic buildup was U.S. closure of the so-called missile gap — a process well underway, and visible to the Soviets before Cuba.[27]

Even in its heyday, however, the "missile gap" defied meaningful definition. To some it symbolized the specter of actual Soviet strategic superiority, while others used the phrase as a rallying cry in opposition to the defense policies of the Eisenhower Administration. In the end, one is left with a mechanistic explanation of the strategic arms competition. In short, the arms race hypothesis tends to muddle, rather than clarify, the political motivations of the participants.

Why, then, did President Kennedy authorize such a rapid expansion of American strategic nuclear power? Mr. McNamara avoided a direct answer to the question in his first annual report as Secretary of Defense: "The need for a rapid build-up of our ballistic missile strength as a matter of highest national priority was confirmed by the 1961 review."[28] McNamara's candor increased considerably, however, six months before his resignation. Speaking to the editors and publishers of United Press International on September 18, 1967, McNamara explained:

> In 1961 when I became Secretary of Defense the Soviet Union had a very small operational arsenal of intercontinental missiles. However, it did possess the technological and industrial capacity to enlarge that arsenal very substantially over the succeeding several years. We had no evidence that the Soviets did plan, in fact, fully to use that capability.[29]

Nevertheless, the Secretary of Defense decided that prudence demanded "a major build-up of our own Minuteman and Polaris forces" because of the administration's uncertainty about Soviet intentions. "But the blunt fact remains that if we had had more accurate information about planned Soviet strategic forces, we simply would not have needed to build as large a nuclear force as we have today." These decisions, McNamara conceded, "could not possibly have left un-affected the Soviet Union's future nuclear plans." The cause of this competition is "that the Soviet Union and the United States mutually influence one another's strategic plans." In the absence of an agreement to limit strategic arms, McNamara concluded that the actions on either side would continue to trigger dangerous reactions on the other side.[30]

The evidence presented in this chapter suggests the following conclusions: In the first place, President Kennedy and his senior national security advisors were aware that the Soviets possessed far fewer ICBMs than previously claimed. To fail to bolster U.S. military power, despite Mr. Kennedy's strident condemnation of the "missile gap" during the campaign, threatened to leave the president open to the charge that he manufactured the entire issue. Indeed, Mr. Kennedy's political ambitions strongly influenced his view of the controversy. Nonetheless, Kennedy and McNamara moved ahead to strengthen the U.S. strategic nuclear deterrent for three reasons: First, to improve the survival of these forces; second, to garner immediate diplomatic advantages for the United States; and third, to persuade the Soviets to accept an American definition of strategic stability based on the mutual vulnerability of their respective societies.

Kennedy's Strategic Forces Statement

Four months after the U-2 incident, an Air Force C-119 transport flying over the South Pacific near Hawaii managed to snare in its trailing Y-shaped net a three-hundred-pound capsule ejected minutes before by the Discoverer-14 satellite. Two additional successful recoveries of film were made before January 1961.[31] It was this program that would provide an accurate count on Soviet ICBMs.

In December 1960, two senior advisors to the president-elect, Jerome B. Wiesner and Walt W. Rostow, attended a Pugwash Conference in Moscow and met with Deputy Foreign Minister V.V. Kuznetsov for three hours. The topics discussed included the release of the two RB-47 crewmen, Berlin and disarmament. During the course of these talks, Kuznetsov expressed his concern over the campaign furor caused by the "missile gap" controversy. He warned his visitors not to expect the Soviet Union to stand still if the new administration went forward with a massive rearmament effort.[32]

On January 31, 1961, Kennedy received an urgent cable from his ambassador in Moscow. Llewellyn Thompson was becoming "increasingly convinced we are grossly overestimating Soviet military strength relative to our own." He urged President Kennedy and Secretary Rusk to be particularly mindful of Soviet sensibilities in their management of the Samos program. "If [the] Soviets [are] as relatively weak militarily as I suspect," Thompson observed, "their reaction to Samos . . . would be quite different than if they are as strong as we give them credit for."[33]

The same day, January 31, 1961, the U.S. Air Force successfully launched an Atlas-Agena A rocket with a Samos II photo-reconnaissance satellite aboard from Point Arguello, California. The satellite transmitted its images to several ground stations by radio signal. Because this technique produced a picture of low quality, Samos was used primarily for area surveillance of the Soviet Union and other Communist countries, and the Discoverer satellites were used to take a closer look from lower orbits.[34]

The technical characteristics of the Samos satellite limited its effective life span to thirty days, and the processing of its photographs probably didn't begin until the end of February 1961.[35] However, the new administration did have access to the output of the fall 1960 Discoverer launches. On February 6, 1961, Secretary McNamara disclosed to reporters during a background briefing that preliminary studies by the administration indicated that there was no "missile gap" in favor of the Soviets. The political uproar was immediate. The next day, White House Press Secretary Pierre Salinger stated that the published reports of Mr. McNamara's interview were "absolutely wrong." Mr. Kennedy faced reporters on the morning of 7 February and repeated McNamara's public denial that "no study had been concluded in the Defense Department which would lead to any conclusion at this time as to whether there is a missile gap or not."[36] The Republican congressional leadership remained incredulous. Senate Majority Leader Everett M. Dirksen remarked caustically that Mr. Kennedy had belabored the Eisenhower Administration with charges that the Republicans had permitted a "missile gap" but, on becoming president, he had been unable to find the gap.[37]

Kennedy received a briefing on Soviet ballistic missile developments from CIA Director Allen Dulles on February 25, 1961.[38] The Dulles presentation presumably included findings from the fall Discoverer launches and possibly some preliminary interpretations of the Samos II images. Nevertheless, the president submitted a special message to Congress, as he promised during the campaign, that justified an increase in spending on strategic ballistic missiles, in part on the judgment that ". . . this nation has not led the world in missile strength."[39] At that moment, the first Polaris submarine, USS *George Washington*, was on-station, the Minuteman missile was successfully flight-tested, and twelve Atlas-D ICBMs were deployed.

The 28 March 1961 message opened with an overview of the president's policy objectives for national defense. "The primary purpose of our arms is peace, not war — to make certain that they will never have to be used — to deter all wars, general or limited, nuclear or conventional, large or small — to convince all potential aggressors that any attack would be futile — to provide backing for diplomatic settlement of disputes — to insure the adequacy of our bargaining power for an end to the arms race." Kennedy then specified his view of the requirements for nuclear deterrence. "Our strategic arms and defenses must be adequate to deter any deliberate nuclear attack on the United States or our allies — by making clear to any potential aggressor that sufficient retaliatory forces will be able to survive a first strike and penetrate his defenses in order to inflict unacceptable losses upon him." Such a force posture, he stressed, must be flexible and determined. "Any potential aggressor contemplating an attack on any part of the Free World . . . must know that our response will be suitable, selective, swift and effective."[40] Mr. Kennedy requested congressional approval of additional funds for FY 1962 to increase the procurement rate of Polaris submarines, to double the production capacity of Minuteman missiles, and to increase the number of B-52 and B-47 bombers on strip alert and place one-eighth of the force on airborne alert at any time.[41]

Secretary McNamara appeared before the House Subcommittee on Defense Appropriations in April 1961 to defend the administration's budget requests for FY 1962. On the opening day of cross-examination, the subcommittee's Democratic chairman, Congressman George Mahan, offered Mr. McNamara an opportunity to explain the administration's position on the "missile gap." McNamara side-stepped the question and claimed that, although a "missile gap" presently existed, the U.S. would have more strategic missiles than the Soviet Union by the end of 1963. McNamara, however, denied the existence of a "deterrence gap," i.e., the inability of the U.S. to respond to a Soviet attack.[42]

McNamara was more candid about the relationship between his own planning assumptions and Soviet missile developments during a subsequent exchange with Congressman Gerald Ford.

Mr. Ford: But if we had a 25 percent downgrading in the Soviet Union ICBM threat within the next several months, that would have a substantial impact on their total destructive force as far as we are concerned?

Secretary McNamara: Yes.

Mr. Ford: If that took place, would that have much impact, if any, on the program you are submitting to us?

Secretary McNamara: It would have some but not much.

Mr. Ford: That is all?[43]

The Reasons

• **Domestic Politics** In a seminal study of the Kennedy Administration's strategic missile program, Desmond Ball concluded that the force expansion was caused by a "combination of perceived economic necessities and the self-generated and intramural bureaucratic pressures..."[44] The derivation of the final force figures of 1,000 Minuteman ICBM launchers and 656 SLBM launchers aboard 41 Polaris submarines was the result, he argues, of a bargaining process between McNamara and the senior officers of the Air Force and Navy. Ball suggests that "...[domestic] political factors would have made it difficult for McNamara and Kennedy to hold the U.S. missile program back even after the demise of the missile gap." Furthermore, he contends that estimates of Soviet missile strength had no influence on the character of the build-up, and the administration's own strategic policies were no more than a rationalization for the original missile decisions.[45]

A prompt and public disavowal of the "missile gap" would have required more political courage than anyone in the administration, to include Kennedy, was willing to muster. The president, for one, had no doubt that the Republicans would take him to task during the next quadrennial contest for his strident espousal of the missile gap in 1960. During the fall of 1961, the president dropped a cloak of secrecy around the U.S. satellite reconnaissance program. Kennedy's motive, according to Philip Klass, was to avoid an open affront to the Soviets that might provoke them into developing the means to destroy U.S. reconnaissance satellites.[46] However, there was also a distinctly partisan reason behind Kennedy's concern with the protection of intelligence information. In July 1962, during a presentation to the National Security Council of the annual National Intelligence Estimate on Soviet Long-Range Attack Capabilities, Kennedy expressed his concern with the relatively widespread distribution of this estimate within the government. He instructed CIA Director John McCone to hold the number of copies to a minimum in the hope that the figures in the estimate could be kept out of the press.[47]

In February 1963 Kennedy began to press his National Security Advisor, McGeorge Bundy, for an analysis of the "missile gap" controversy. He wanted to "know its genesis; what previous government officials put forth their views and how we came to the judgment that there was a missile gap."[48] On 4 March, McNamara forwarded a memorandum to the president on the "missile gap" controversy prepared by one of his assistants, Adam Yarmolinsky. The Yarmolinsky report argued that "Whatever may be said (in hindsight) of the reality of the 'missile gap,' there is no question about the reality of a 'defense gap' which required vigorous action by the incoming Administration to correct." The report concluded that "the missile gap was based on a comparison between U.S. ICBM strength as then programmed, and reasonable, although erroneous, estimates of prospective Soviet ICBM strength which were generally accepted by responsible officials."[49] Bundy was not satisfied with the report, and he asked Yarmolinsky to provide "more on the immediate period when we said there was *no* missile gap — December 1960–February 1961."[50]

Bundy, of course, was particularly sensitive to the continued fallout from McNamara's assertion in February 1961 that the "missile gap" had disappeared. Yarmolinsky tried his hand again in a 15 March memo to Bundy. He stated that "the difference between Mr. McNamara denying there was a gap and the Eisenhower Administration saying the same thing ... is this: Under Eisenhower, the denial that there was no gap was accompanied by a belief, at the highest levels, that our defense posture was adequate; under the new Administration, the denial was accompanied by an intense awareness that, although we were not in immediate great danger, urgent immediate steps were nevertheless needed to improve our defense position." Yarmolinsky closed on the theme he developed in his previous report. "Thus, although there was little difference in what Defense officials *said* about the missile gap before and after January 1961, there were major differences in what was *done* about the missile gap and the whole range of defense deficiencies which this term had come to symbolize."[51]

Bundy, however, hesitated in sending the Yarmolinsky report and addendum to the president. Bundy received a note on 30 March from the president's naval aide, Commander Tazewell Shepard. Once again the president inquired about the status of the "missile gap" study, and he also wanted included an appraisal of the military and space deficiencies which existed in January 1961 together with an *ex post facto* justification for the steps required to overcome these deficiencies. Kennedy finally received the Defense Department's report in mid–May and he found the analysis to be "too superficial." "I want to be able to demonstrate," Kennedy stated, "that there was a military and intelligence lag in the previous administration that started the missile gap."[52]

Paul Nitze, the Assistant Secretary of Defense for International Security Affairs, also tried to meet the President's request. The report was prepared by Nitze's special assistant, Lawrence C. McQuade. McQuade concluded that the "missile gap" turned out to be a "dud." However, "In light of the circumstances as they looked during the period of the late 1950s, the missile gap was a serious phenomenon calling for significant shifts in our defense posture to decrease U.S. vulnerability."[53] Nitze's own comments on the "missile gap" remain instructive. The entire issue seemed to Nitze to be much ado about nothing: "In fact, his [Kennedy's] program for action made sense whether or not the intelligence on the Soviet ICBM program was accurate."[54]

• **Diplomatic Leverage** Despite subsequent denials, the diplomatic utility of strategic nuclear power was of particular concern to the Kennedy Administration.[55] A popular scenario of the "missile gap" era was one in which an American president might confront the Soviets in some future crisis and face the choice of suicide or surrender. A successful Soviet counterforce strike against U.S. strategic nuclear forces would present the president or his designated successor with a stark choice: Should he fire the remaining U.S. weapons against Soviet cities and receive a devastating response in kind, or should he simply surrender? This scenario had an important effect on Kennedy and McNamara and directly influenced their decision to construct a force posture based on surviving reserve forces capable of dominating a nuclear battlefield no matter how hollow the victory. Such a wartime capability also offered important diplomatic dividends in peacetime.

Khrushchev's rhetorical support of wars of national liberation throughout the Third World became one of the principal justifications for major increases in U.S. conventional and counter-insurgency capabilities. However, here too nuclear weapons played an important role. This was a mirror image of the Kennedy Administration's perception of Soviet strategic intentions. According to McNamara,

> We must continue to provide for forces required to deter an all-out nuclear war. Only behind the shield of such forces can the free world hope to cope successfully with lesser military aggression.... The ability to respond promptly to limited aggression, possibly in more than one place at a time, can serve both to deter them and to prevent them from spreading out into larger conflicts.[56]

McNamara's second objective was to raise the escalation threshold. "The escalation to a higher level of war is probably more likely to occur if we go into these limited actions 'ill equipped and ill prepared' to support the political positions and political objectives that have previously been established."[57]

From mid-June to mid-September 1961, four capsules containing reconnaissance photographs were recovered from Discoverer satellites.[58] These recoveries were followed by the drastic downgrading of the national estimate of operational Soviet ICBMs in mid-September 1961. NIE 11-8-61, issued on June 7, 1961, stated the Soviets might already have 50 to 100 operational ICBM launchers by mid-1961 and they would have 100-200 operational launchers within the next year. On September 21, 1961, the United States Intelligence Board issued a revision of the June estimate based on the summer satellite coverage. The official estimate of Soviet ICBMs on launchers turned out to be a meager 10-25, with no marked increase considered likely during the immediately succeeding months. By mid-1963 the expected number of Soviet ICBMs was 75-125.[59]

These figures were apparently corroborated by materials provided to the CIA by Colonel Oleg Penkovskiy. During the late spring of 1961, Penkovskiy turned over to U.S. officials three installments of microfilm on the number of Soviet missiles deployed, highly technical information on the difficulties the Soviets encountered with the SS-6, and excerpts from the minutes of those top-level meetings where it was decided to scrap the program.[60]

On October 22, 1961, five days after Khrushchev withdrew his Berlin deadline, Deputy Secretary of Defense Roswell Gilpatric addressed the Business Council at Hot Springs, Virginia. Gilpatric's speech marked the beginning of a massive campaign of psychological pressure by the Kennedy Administration to warn Mr. Khrushchev not to trifle with the United States and to educate the Soviet military about the "subtleties" of nuclear strategy. Gilpatric stated that the Soviet Union's "Iron Curtain is not so impenetrable as to force us to accept at face value the Kremlin boasts." He warned that the U.S. "has the nuclear retaliatory force of such lethal powers that an enemy move which brought it into play would be an act of self-destruction." Gilpatric then provided the most comprehensive statement of U.S. capabilities to date. He stated that SAC possessed a fleet of 600 long-range B-52 bombers, even more of the shorter-range B-47s, the Navy's six Polaris submarines with a total of 96 missiles and the several dozen Atlas missiles then operational.[61]

The following day, Secretary of State Rusk appeared on the ABC network's program "Issues and Answers" to make sure Khrushchev did not miss the political message contained in Gilpatric's remarks. The main point of the speech, according to Rusk, was the fact that the U.S. could defeat the Soviet Union in a nuclear war even if they struck the first blow. Consequently, Rusk declared that the U.S. was not "dealing in the world ... from a position of weakness." Mr. Rusk added that he had "no doubt" that Premier Khrushchev had a "very accurate assessment" of American strength.[62] McNamara amplified Gilpatric's remarks in a speech in Atlanta on 11 November in which he gave a litany of the administration's accomplishments during the past ten months "to strengthen and protect our nuclear strength."[63]

McNamara carried this message to Congress during his presentation in January 1962 of the Defense Department's FY 1963 budget. Citing Khrushchev's January 1961 speech in support of wars of national liberation as evidence of Soviet aggressiveness, McNamara concluded, "I see no reason to assume that we will face anything other than a continuation of Cold War.... I have every reason to believe he [Khrushchev] was outlining very clearly his objectives and his plans for accomplishing them, and I think we must anticipate we will face more and more of that in the years to come.... We must continue to convince him [Khrushchev] that thermonuclear war would destroy the Soviet Union and therefore that he should refrain from actions that would bring on such wars."[64]

• **Strategic Stability** A subtle but significant shift in U.S. strategic policy began to unfold during the summer of 1962. McNamara began to retreat from the "No-Cities" doctrine he marked out in Ann Arbor. The obvious explanation is that the Secretary of Defense found himself on a politically precarious limb and backed quickly to a safer position. He later admitted to his closest aides that his speech might have gone too far in the direction of counterforce.[65] In the opinion of Roswell Gilpatric, the entire notion "evolved in McNamara's mind ... without too much clearance or exchange of views, either within or without the [Defense] department...."[66] The comment suggests that McNamara only dabbled in matters of strategy. As James R. Schlesinger has written, "Shifting sands seems the best way to characterize the strategic rationales" of the period.[67]

There was, however, an eminently reasonable explanation for McNamara beginning to alter his strategic vision. In July 1962 Hanson Baldwin of the *New York Times* reported that the Soviets had begun to deploy their second-generation ICBM, the SS-7, in horizontal concrete coffins.[68] The development was evidence that the Soviets were equally concerned about the vulnerability of their land-based missiles. The Kennedy Administration reasoned that such concern might even indicate that the Soviets would be receptive to further education. McNamara and Kennedy spent the next six months trying to persuade the Soviets to accept an American version of strategic stability: the prevention of accidental war, discriminatory targeting, and no nuclear defenses.

The Limits of Interaction

Four days after President Kennedy's inauguration, a B-52 bomber carrying two 24-megaton gravity bombs had crashed near Goldsboro, North Carolina. Five of the six safety devices on one of the bombs failed.[69] The incident served to heighten the administration's profound concern with the threat of accidental war. In the words of McNamara's deputy, Roswell Gilpatric, the administration was "making sure that something didn't misfire or miscarry, or that some sergeant or squadron leader or somebody else didn't do something which would upset the train and cause a nuclear holocaust."[70]

Soviet command and control technology was extremely primitive during the early 1960s. Their solution to the problem of unauthorized launch was a simple one. Nuclear warheads were stored nearly 50 miles away from missile launch sites. This was probably one of the reasons the Soviet missile force never went on a full alert during the Cuban missile crisis. Kennedy and McNamara took several steps to inform the Soviets about U.S. safety and security procedures in the aftermath of the confrontation. U.S. diplomats began to inform their Soviet counterparts about the operation of permissive action links, i.e., electronic locks for nuclear warheads.[76]

The president authorized John T. McNaughton, the Defense Department's general counsel, to outline the administration's concerns publicly. McNaughton spoke at an arms control symposium at the University of Michigan in December 1962. No matter how politically competitive the Cold War, McNaughton argued that "each side . . . has an interest in avoiding the eruption, escalation or prolongation of nuclear war by accident or miscalculation." This interest, he stated, would be served by three kinds of unilateral military decisions: (1) those designed to prevent war "by accident" — through an unauthorized or unintended firing of a nuclear weapon; (2) those designed to prevent war "by miscalculation" — through lack of time or absence of doctrine to permit deliberate, controlled response, especially in crises;

(3) those designed to reduce the damage should a war occur, by building firebreaks against escalation of conflict, by pursuing a strategy which is antimilitary rather than antipopulation, and by insuring that the power to stop a war is preserved.[72] McNaughton concluded his remarks with the "hope that the Soviet Union is prepared to adopt similar measures for its own security and the security of the world."[73]

The Soviets responded positively to McNaughton's initial recommendation. Deputy Foreign Minister V.V. Kuznetsov showed his awareness of U.S. nuclear security procedures during the course of negotiations in New York with Undersecretary of State George Ball, Adlai Stevenson and Gilpatric on the removal of Soviet IL-28 bombers from Cuba.[74] The Soviets subsequently announced that their missiles were "equipped with a reliable blocking system which can prevent any accident, mistake, or misunderstanding."[75] The Soviets were contemptuous of McNaughton's remaining recommendations. Khrushchev expressed his derision of the notion of miscalculation at the Vienna Summit, and Soviet commentators spared no effort to condemn McNamara's strategy of counterforce. A pamphlet published in 1963 accused "American propaganda" of trying to deceive the "popular masses" on the fact that "to separate military targets from nonmilitary ones in a rocket-nuclear war is difficult since modern weapons possess such power and such characteristics that strikes, inflicted on military targets, will hit cities and other populated points separated from the given targets by hundreds and even thousands of kilometers."[76]

McNamara persisted in his preachments to the Soviets. He told Stewart Alsop that "...a nuclear exchange, confined to military targets seems more possible, not less, when both sides have a sure second strike capability. Then you might have a 'stable balance of terror.'"[77]

The Soviets now began to move towards a kind of direct discourse with Western military analysts. The November 1963 issue of *International Affairs* included an article by I. Glagolev and V. Larionov. Glagolev is a Soviet specialist on international relations, and Colonel Larionov was one of the authors of *Voennaya Strategiya*. This rather interesting collaboration marked a departure from past Soviet practice.[78] Glagolev and Larionov accused foreign military analysts of "talking through their hats" when they said that Soviet nuclear missiles were highly vulnerable and designed mainly for a first strike. The authors went on to make the point that Soviet efforts to disperse, harden, and conceal their forces made it impossible to knock out all these forces simultaneously. Glagolev and Larionov then offered a conclusion at odds with McNamara's own vision of strategic stability:

The first rockets and bombers of the side on the defensive would take off even before the aggressor's first rockets, to say nothing of his bombers, reached their targets.[79]

In the parlance of strategic analysis, the tactic is called launch-on-warning. Glagolev and Larionov had simply refined Khrushchev's crude notion of a push-button war and fashioned an effective rhetorical response to McNamara.

McNamara's persistent espousal of counterforce despite a clear Soviet unwillingness to play by American rules deserves a closer look. McNamara believed strongly that there was no meaningful defense to nuclear weapons. In this sense, his counterforce strategy was no more than an improvisation to impede the development of a meaningful nuclear defense of the United States. McNamara was never enthusiastic about civil defense. According to former Assistant Secretary of Defense Steuart Pittman, the head of the Kennedy civil defense program, McNamara "hardly supported" his own recommendations to the president.[80] In 1963, McNamara suddenly linked civil defense to the deployment of the Nike-X anti-ballistic missile system in his defense budget recommendation for FY 1964. It was McNamara who had previously maintained that the civil defense fallout shelter program could stand on its own merits. The fact that he was approving smaller and smaller amounts for civil defense and linking the program to ABM might suggest that the secretary was engaged in a political gambit to delay ABM indefinitely.[81] The Kennedy Administration, and especially Mr. McNamara, believed that the deployment of a ballistic missile defense against the Soviet Union would be provocative and destabilizing. The system would accomplish little for its cost, it would be vulnerable to various counter-measures such as decoys and penetration aids, and it would accelerate the arms race to higher levels with little gain in security for either side.[82] Dr. Herbert York, a senior Defense official during the Eisenhower and Kennedy years, stated the case against ABM this way:

> The problem here is the usual problem between defense and offense, measures, counter-measures, counter-counter measures, *et cetera*, in which it has been my judgement and still is that the battle is so heavily weighted in favor of the offense that it is hopeless against a determined offense and that incidentally applies to our position with regard to an anti-missile that they [the Soviets] might build. I am convinced that we can continue to have a missile system that can penetrate any Soviet defense.[83]

The Soviet view of defense in the nuclear age was succinctly expressed by the internationally known Soviet physicist, P. Kapitsa.

> In the struggle for the prevention of atomic war it is essential to take into account the possibility that there will be found a reliable defense against nuclear weapons. If this is achieved by a country with aggressive intentions, then being itself protected against the direct effects of nuclear weapons, it can much more easily decide to launch an atomic war.[84]

In 1955, the year before Kapitsa's comments, the Soviets began a new and extensive compulsory civil defense program for the population that included training in the use of shelters, first aid, fire-fighting, and rescue techniques in contaminated areas. In 1960 civil defense responsibilities were transferred from the Ministry of Interior to the Ministry of Defense. The reorganization was matched by greater attention to the evacuation of the population in the event of nuclear war. However, as Leon Goure has noted, "the Soviet Civil Defense System in general puts protective measures for administration, industrial and control institutions [e.g., the KGB] ahead of those for the general population."[85] A debate occurred in 1962 on the direction of civil defense and appeared to be resolved in favor of a vigorous program. In the judgment of Marshal V.I. Chuikov, the civil defense head at the time, "not a single defense measure can be decided under modern conditions without considering civil defense."[86]

Evidence that the Soviets were involved in producing an antiballistic missile began to appear in 1961. Khrushchev told C.L. Sulzberger in September that work on offensive and defensive missiles was going forward simultaneously and satisfactorily.[87] The following month, Marshal Malinovskiy announced at the Twenty-Second Party Congress "that the problem of destroying missiles in flight has also been resolved."[88] Khrushchev went so far as to claim that the Soviet ABM could "hit a fly" in space.[89] The Soviets did not actually display their first ABM until two years later. According to Western estimates, this missile, nicknamed the Griffon by NATO, was first tested in 1962. The eight-ton Griffon was a two-stage missile with an altitude of 25 to 30 miles, a slant range of about 100 miles and a speed of Mach 3 to 5, and could probably be fitted with either a TNT or nuclear warhead. Deployment of the missile began around Leningrad and was suddenly halted. But in 1964 the Soviets began to dismantle these sites. The purpose of the Griffon deployment remains uncertain. Some experts argue that it was deployed as a defense against U.S. Jupiter and Thor missiles based in Britain, Italy, and Turkey. This argument seems unreasonable because those systems were in the process of being dis-

mantled when the Griffon deployment began. A more likely explanation is that the Griffon was a counter to American high-performance
bombers armed with air-to-surface missiles, such as the B-58 and the
projected B-70.[90] The Soviets began to deploy a new ABM missile,
known in the West as the Galosh, around Moscow. The system was
eventually comprised of four complexes, each with target acquisition
radars, tracking radars and sixteen launchers. The Galosh missile
itself is a slow-reacting, thirty-six-ton missile designed to engage incoming warheads several hundred miles above the earth.

One of the more important justifications for the Soviet ABM was
provided by Major General Talenskiy:

> From the standpoint of strategy, powerful deterrent forces and an
> effective anti-missile defense system ... substantially increase the
> stability of mutual deterrence from any partial shifts in the qualita-
> tive and quantitative balance of these two component elements of
> mutual deterrence.... After all, when the security of a state is
> based only on mutual deterrence with the aid of powerful nuclear
> rockets, it is directly dependent on the good will and designs of the
> other side, which is a highly subjective and indefinite factor.[91]

McNamara spent the next several years opposing the deployment
of an ABM system in the United States and trying to show the Soviets
the error of their ways. By late 1966, congressional conservatives were
prepared to authorize appropriations for an ABM deployment despite
McNamara's opposition. The ABM had now become a rallying point
for those in the House and Senate who also demanded that the Johnson Administration increase American defense spending and win the
war in Vietnam. During a series of meetings at the Texas White House
in December, McNamara reportedly persuaded President Johnson to
"hold off" his decision on the Sentinel ABM system until a final attempt was made "to get the Soviet Union to turn this thing around."
Johnson agreed to couple a plea to the Soviets for negotiations on
strategic weapons to a request to Congress for $375 million. The funds
were earmarked for a "possible" ABM deployment if diplomacy
failed.[92] Johnson convened a formal meeting at the White House on
January 4, 1967, to discuss the ABM issue with a "blue ribbon" panel
composed of the Joint Chiefs of Staff, all former presidential science
advisors as well as all previous assistant secretaries of defense for
research and development. The scientists present were unanimous in
their opposition to the deployment of an ABM system.[93]

McNamara's final opportunity to ease congressional pressure
came six months later. The occasion was a meeting between the

President and Soviet Premier Aleksei Kosygin at Glassboro, New Jersey. At a London press conference in February 1967, Kosygin reaffirmed the Soviet Union's intention to complete the construction of the ABM launch sites to defend Moscow. In Kosygin's opinion, "...a defensive system, which prevents attack, is not a cause of the arms race but represents a factor preventing the death of people."[94]

McNamara rushed to the June meeting at Glassboro with his briefing notes in hand. Neither side, he told Kosygin, could hope to achieve a meaningful superiority in nuclear arms. The ABM, he continued, was a threat to the stability of the strategic balance. Kosygin remained adamantly opposed to any compromise. He chided McNamara about being an "arms merchant," and sanctimoniously declared Soviet interest in defensive as opposed to offensive weapons.[95] In the aftermath of Glassboro, Johnson directed his Secretary of Defense to yield on ABM. Four months later, McNamara announced the president's decision to deploy "a relatively light and reliable Chinese-oriented ABM system" at an estimated cost exceeding $5 billion. The Sentinel system was to provide area protection for the twenty-five largest cities in the U.S. with short-range Sprint missiles and longer-range Spartan missiles, both armed with thermonuclear warheads. In the end, McNamara conjured the least plausible justification for a strategy he bitterly opposed.

Implications for the Strategic Competition

The apparent divergence in Soviet and American attitudes towards civil defense and ballistic missile defense would suggest equally different approaches to the problem of deterrence. McNamara clearly championed the threat of unacceptable punishment to deter a Soviet nuclear attack. Senior Soviet military officers were equally vigorous in their assertion that the Soviet Union would prevail on the nuclear battlefield. This dichotomy between deterrence and defense, however, is not as obvious as one might suspect. Khrushchev revealed in his memoirs that his enthusiastic claims about the performance of the Soviet ABM program had little to do with the truth.

> I used to say sometimes in my speeches that we had developed an antimissile missile that could hit a fly, but of course that was just rhetoric to make our adversaries think twice. In fact, it is impossible to intercept incoming ICBM's with pinpoint accuracy and total reliability; even if you knock down most of them, a few are bound to get through.[96]

The ability to bring the United States itself under fire was what mattered most to Khrushchev. This, in his view, was the essence of deterrence and the reason the United States could not risk an attack on the Soviet Union. "I'm not complaining," he wrote, "as long as the President understands that even though he may be able to destroy us two times over, we're still capable of wiping out the United States, even if it's only once."[97]

This point was completely lost on President Kennedy and Mr. McNamara. Numbers did matter to them. Khrushchev was in part to blame for this. His inflated rhetoric in the aftermath of Sputnik and subsequent claims of military superiority energized the Kennedy Administration and provided an opportune justification for the expansion of U.S. strategic nuclear forces. There is no evidence, however, that the administration seriously considered the effect this policy would have on the Soviet Union. This oversight was not the product of ignorance, but arrogance. McNamara was certain that the Soviet Union would simply concede the United States' advantage in the strategic arms race. He confidently assured the members of the House Subcommittee on Defense Appropriations in February 1963 that U.S. strategic superiority was secure.

> The Soviets could, over the next few years build a large force of hardened second generation ICBMs; they could develop and deploy an ICBM delivery system for the large yield nuclear warheads they have been testing since 1961; they could expand and improve their active defenses against manned bomber attack; they could maintain a large and modernly equipped army; they could develop and deploy some sort of a system of active defense against ballistic missile attack; they could modernize and improve their large fleet of submarines, including ballistic missile firing types; they could continue the space race, they could expand both military and economic aid to the non-aligned nations; they could make the great investment needed to create an efficient agricultural economy; they could continue to push the development of heavy industry; or they could increase the standard of living of the Soviet people — *but they cannot do them all at the same time.*[98]

One member of the committee did not share McNamara's confident appraisal. Representative Melvin Laird expressed his concerns in a letter to President Kennedy on January 19, 1963, and later added the letter to the record of McNamara's testimony in February. Laird pointedly asked the president, "If a more stable balance of terror by the expedient of permitting the Soviet Union to develop an adequate second strike capability is now the wish of the United States, my question is: what strategy will we pursue when that happens. . . . If, as a superior power, we pursue 'the underdog strategy,' Mr. President, what strategy will we pursue when we are 'equidogs'? When nuclear parity has become a fact."[99]

President Kennedy found himself on the horns of a dilemma. On the one hand, he attempted to make nuclear war unthinkable by setting the upper bound of the strategic equation. U.S. strategic superiority was viewed as a panacea that would deter the spectrum of Soviet military threats to American security interests world-wide. On the other hand, the president tried to construct a modicum of strategic stability with the Kremlin tethered to a professed belief in parity. Tragically, however, neither he nor his advisors appreciated the inherent contradiction between these two objectives and the political implications of nuclear parity on the superpower relationship.

Chapter 4

Alliance Politics and Nuclear Independence

Alliances, to be sure, are good, but forces of one's own are better.
Frederick William of Brandenburg

The Erosion of Bipolarity

The prevailing pattern of Cold War politics began to change in the late 1950s. Newfound prosperity and a resurgence in national pride in Western Europe combined to challenge America's postwar predominance on the continent. The principal instigator was General Charles de Gaulle. There were neither permanent allies nor implacable enemies on the world stage, according to the Gaullist perspective — only persistent threats to the independence of France and to the expansion of its global power and prestige. The general's politics left no room for altruistic behavior. It mattered little to de Gaulle that France benefitted from the military strength of the North Atlantic Alliance. If the alliance's policy conflicted with French vital interests, the former was expected to yield.[1] However, political independence in the absence of commensurate military capabilities was a hollow virtue to General de Gaulle. The grandeur and security of France demanded a nuclear deterrent of its own — the *force de frappe*.

The first public fissures in the Sino-Soviet alliance appeared in 1960, and the differences between the powers grew sharper in the three years that followed. What mattered most to Nikita Khrushchev, as well as Mao Zedong, was national power, not ideology. If anything, the dispute demonstrated just how imprecise and misleading Marxism-Leninism really is, providing ample support for any number of conflicting and contradictory policy positions. The reasons for the controversy were more fundamental. The Soviet Union was a "satisfied"

87

power with a stake in the international status quo. Communist China was a thoroughly "dissatisfied power" with its lost province of Taiwan in the hands of Chiang K'ai-shek. The Chinese revolution was only a decade old and its leader a revolutionary figure of historic proportions. The Russian Revolution was as middle-aged as its erstwhile leader. Khrushchev's difficulty came in persuading his allies, especially the Chinese, that on certain matters and at certain times, the Soviets would have to make decisions on their own without consulting with their allies.[2] Khrushchev may have expected the Chinese to come to the defense of the Soviet Union in time of war, but he certainly had no intention of leading the Soviet people to war to protect Mao's brand of Communist revolution.

The appearance of new constellations of power in 1963 led one prominent journalist to suggest that the East-West relations of the future "could make the past years of simple Cold War — of one against one look easy."[3] As France and Communist China pulled away from their respective political orbits, the United States and the Soviet Union were drawn closer together by a common concern with the dangers of nuclear proliferation and a common interest in protecting their duopolistic dominance of world affairs. The United States attempted to meet the military aspirations of its allies with a diplomatic sleight-of-hand known as the Multilateral Force. Khrushchev, to his regret, agreed to support the Chinese nuclear program in 1957 in exchange for Beijing's condemnation of Yugoslav revisionism. Khrushchev balked less than two years later when the Chinese asked for a copy of a Soviet nuclear weapon, and he promptly terminated Soviet assistance.

Most interpretations of the East-West detente that flowered during the summer of 1963 point to Kennedy's and Khrushchev's common experiences at the brink of war during the Cuban missile crisis. Both leaders certainly came away from the crisis with a renewed sense of responsibility and a sober appreciation of the dangers of unmitigated hostility between their two countries. The evidence presented in this chapter suggests, however, that the emergence of a more collaborative relationship was primarily a product of their mutual fear of nuclear proliferation in general, and of Communist China in particular. Premier Khrushchev began years earlier to call for a sweeping deal by which Moscow and Washington would jointly police the world and monopolize nuclear weapons. But his price for an agreement to end nuclear testing and to forbid the transfer of nuclear know-how was always considered by the United States to be greedy and strategically one-sided.[4] Communist China's hostile rhetoric changed his mind as well as President Kennedy's. The final negotiations leading to a

Limited Nuclear Test Ban Treaty became the vehicle for their collaboration.

The transition from a bipolar to a multipolar world during the early 1960s came as no surprise to Raymond Aron. "The idea that the two great powers of an international system are brothers at the same time as being enemies should be accepted as banal rather than paradoxical." The logic of this assertion was quite obvious to him. "Each prefers to preserve the thermonuclear duopoly rather than allow the dissemination of weapons of mass destruction, both fear total war more than the limited advance of their rival."[5] Even Aron probably would have been surprised to learn the depth of President Kennedy's fear of a nuclear China and his willingness to contemplate the use of military force to prevent that eventuality. Mao certainly angered Khrushchev, but not enough to collaborate with the United States against another Communist power.

NATO's Nuclear Shield: The First Ten Years

The Eisenhower Administration wasted no time in applying the precepts of massive retaliation to the defense of Western Europe. In May 1954 the NATO Council directed the Supreme Allied Commander, Europe (SACEUR) to base NATO's tactical defense on nuclear weapons. NATO's military staff spent the next three years formulating an appropriate strategy. The North Atlantic Council endorsed a plan for the nuclear defense of Europe, entitled MC-70, in May 1957 along with the introduction of U.S.-controlled tactical nuclear warheads. Conventional forces according to this plan were to serve as merely a trip wire in the event of a Soviet-led invasion by the Warsaw Pact. The full power of the Strategic Air Command and NATO's theater nuclear forces would be used against the enemy once the intra-German border was crossed.

NATO's principal European members—Great Britain, France, and the German Federal Republic—were enthusiastic supporters of a nuclear defense of Europe. This strategy offered several obvious advantages. The greater the American nuclear commitment, the more closely the United States was perceived by its allies to be tied to Europe's defense. Furthermore, the strategy contributed to their economic growth by minimizing the need for substantial manpower and material resources otherwise required for a conventional defense. Chancellor Adenauer and his Defense Minister Franz Josef Strauss were among its most vocal supporters. Both believed that a lower nuclear threshold would add to Soviet political uncertainties and increase the credibility of NATO. Although West Germany was prohibited by the 1954 Paris Accords from producing biological, chemical or nuclear weapons of its own, NATO's two-key control system allowed Bonn to enjoy vicariously the status of a nuclear power, much to the Kremlin's dismay. The two-key system was designed to meet the restrictions imposed by the Atomic Energy Act of 1946, the so-called McMahon Act, that prohibited the United States from turning over to a foreign government the control of U.S. nuclear warheads. The U.S. retained control of nuclear warheads assigned to NATO while the participating nations owned the delivery systems — missiles, aircraft and/or atomic artillery.

Sputnik I and the subsequent controversy surrounding the alleged "missile gap" had an insidious effect on the confidence and morale of America's European allies. If Soviet missiles were now capable of bringing the U.S. homeland under attack, Europeans asked, what guarantee did *they* have that an American president would risk the destruction of his own country to defend Europe? The Eisenhower Administration's military reaction was to launch the Polaris missile program, and its political response was to reassure America's NATO allies. The North Atlantic Council agreed in principle in December 1957 to a U.S. plan to deploy intermediate range ballistic missiles in Europe. The following year, the Eisenhower Administration gained congressional approval for an amendment to the McMahon Act to permit joint control of these weapons and to mate the warheads to the missiles. The deployment of sixty Thor missiles in Great Britain began in 1959, and that year agreements were also reached with Italy and Turkey to deploy a total of forty-five Jupiter missiles. The deployment of these missiles was also expected to satisfy European calls for greater integration of the alliance's military forces. The call for integration was actually a demand for greater allied participation in the decisions affecting the planned employment of NATO's nuclear forces. While the leaders of the French Fourth Republic were content to live with U.S. political control of NATO's nuclear forces, le Grande Charles was not.

General Charles de Gaulle became the Fifth Republic's first president in June 1958, and he wasted no time informing his allies and the world that he had every intention of restoring France to its proper place in world affairs. In September he told President Eisenhower and Prime Minister Macmillan that the French Mediterranean Fleet was no longer under NATO's command and that he would not permit the deployment of any NATO nuclear weapon system on French soil unless France was given control of the warheads; finally, he urged both leaders to join with France to form a tripartite directorate within NATO to determine alliance policy world-wide. Moreover, de Gaulle informed both leaders that France intended to develop its own nuclear deterrent. De Gaulle outlined his rationale for the *force de frappe* at a Paris news conference two months later:

> Who can say that in the future, the political background having changed completely – that is something that has already happened on earth – the two powers having the nuclear monopoly will not agree to divide the world? Who can say that if the occasion arises the two, while each deciding not to launch its missiles at the main enemy so that it should itself be spared, will not crush the others? It is possible to imagine on some awful day Western Europe should be wiped out from Moscow and Central Europe from Washington. And who can even say that the two rivals, after I know not what political and social upheaval, will not unite?[6]

De Gaulle saw the superpowers being pulled in two contradictory directions: either towards war and annihilation or towards a mutual accord and condominial rule of the international system. A Soviet-American condominium was as much a threat to France as global war. A condominium would weaken the legal and moral authority of third nations to provide for the security and solvency of their populace. However, the balance of terror offered Gaullist France an unparalleled opportunity to pursue a foreign policy independent of either superpower. The *force de frappe* was an indispensable prop in de Gaulle's global diplomacy. France exploded its first atomic device on February 13, 1960, in the Saharan desert.

NATO's Secretary-General Paul Henri Spaak, Chancellor Konrad Adenauer, and General Lauris Norstad, SACEUR, were instrumental in urging the members of the alliance to fashion an alternative to President de Gaulle's national deterrent. Speaking before the annual conference of NATO parliamentarians in November, General Norstad urged the North Atlantic Alliance to take "a great and dramatic new step" by agreeing to form a NATO-controlled nuclear force. The conference adopted a resolution that it was "urgent and essential" to study this proposal. The following month, Secretary of State Christian Herter endorsed the "concept" of a NATO MRBM force composed of five Polaris submarines armed with eighty missiles to be deployed before 1963, contingent upon an agreed "multilateral system" of control acceptable to the United States, and the purchase of one hundred additional Polaris missiles by NATO from the U.S. to be deployed on a fleet of surface ships. There was considerable uncertainty, especially in Great Britain, about the feasibility of sharing the decision to use nuclear weapons among the fifteen member states; put more graphically, it was a danger of "fifteen fingers on the trigger."

Kennedy, de Gaulle and Nuclear Independence

Kennedy gave his tacit support to a NATO nuclear force during the 1960 presidential campaign. "It would be uneconomic and unwise," he warned, "for each of our partners to build a wholly independent nuclear system." Instead, Kennedy endorsed "arrangements . . . to contribute to the deterrence of nuclear war, without increasing the instability of the military position and without wasting European resources in the futile efforts of each nation to create its own nuclear weapons and delivery capabilities."[7]

Kennedy stressed, at the outset of his incumbency, that he intended to explore the possibilities of a new and more flexible military strategy to deter general nuclear war as well as any Soviet attack on NATO, no matter how limited in scope. The new administration's defense proposals were intended to secure, as rapidly as possible, strategic nuclear superiority over the Soviets; substantially increase NATO's conventional forces, particularly by the alliance's European members; and raise the threshold at which a Soviet conventional attack on NATO would be met with tactical and strategic nuclear weapons.

On April 10, 1961, Kennedy addressed NATO's Military Council at the opening session of its meeting in Washington. The president told the representatives that "NATO needs to be able to respond to any conventional attack with conventional resistance which will be effective at least long enough, in General Norstad's phrase, to 'force a pause.'"[8] The previous November Norstad had stated that in the event of large-scale fighting in Europe, which he envisaged as the product of miscalculation or "momentary rashness," NATO forces would "enforce a pause" in the hope that diplomacy could avert the recourse to strategic arms.[9] The new ideas of the Kennedy Administration, however, went beyond Norstad's concept. The SACEUR sought a doctrine to rationalize NATO's existing force structure; the Kennedy Administration wanted to change fundamentally the mission of these forces.[10] The direction of this change was spelled out in a National Security Council Directive entitled *NATO and the Atlantic Nations*, approved by President Kennedy on April 21, 1961. The directive contained the principal recommendations of a study prepared by former Secretary of State Dean Acheson. The United States was to give the "highest priority" to raising the manning levels, modernizing the equipment, and improving the mobility of NATO's non-nuclear forces. No European member of the alliance would be permitted to exercise a veto over the use of U.S. strategic forces assigned to the theater, and the nuclear forces of the other members should be subject to a U.S. veto and control.[11]

President de Gaulle remained adamantly opposed to the new thrust of American military strategy. During a Paris news conference on April 11, 1961, de Gaulle stated:

> It is the duty and the right ... of European powers to have their own national defense. It is intolerable to a great nation that its destiny be left to the decisions ... of another nation however friendly.[12]

In the opinion of General Ailleret, the Chief of Staff of the French Armed Forces, a conventional response to a Soviet invasion would fail because of NATO's shortage of non-nuclear capabilities. Tactical nuclear weapons were an "incredible" option because their use "would completely wipe out Europe over a depth of eighteen hundred miles from the Atlantic to the Soviet frontier." The only credible deterrent to Soviet aggression was "immediate strategic action"—in Ailleret's words, "Destroying the root of that aggression and its chance of drawing strength, by dropping strategic nuclear bombs on the war potential of the country unleashing the aggression and thus causing that country to give up its aggression."[13] Consequently, the French General Staff showed no interest in such issues as maintenance of communications between the hostile sides, control over the amount of force to be employed, limits on damage to civilian population centers, and the swift termination of hostilities.

The U.S. offer of five Polaris submarines to SACEUR was reiterated by Secretary of State Rusk on 8 May in Oslo at the annual spring meeting of NATO's foreign ministers. The plan outlined by Rusk, however, was substantially different from the one originally proposed by the Eisenhower Administration six months earlier. The U.S. reportedly would assign the Polaris boats to American-commanded units currently committed to NATO defense tasks. This new plan did not include the original proposals for joint control of the submarines or for European purchases of one hundred Polaris missiles to be stockpiled for the submarines' use. Rusk coupled the plan to a renewed U.S. appeal for European action to strengthen NATO's conventional forces. President Kennedy publicized the U.S. offer during a speech in Ottawa on May 17, 1961. He told the Canadian Parliament that the defense requirements of the 1960s required NATO to strengthen its conventional capabilities and "make certain that nuclear weapons will continue to be available . . . and under close and flexible political control that meets the needs of all NATO countries." He also tied the offer of five Polaris submarines to the achievement of NATO's non-nuclear force goals, and he held out the "possibility of eventually establishing a NATO sea-borne missile force which would be truly multilateral in ownership and control. . . ."[14]

German Defense Minister Franz Josef Strauss, for one, was highly critical of the new turn in American defense policy. He declared that West Germany "adheres to the policy of [the nuclear] deterrent" and that his task was to insure that "the credibility of this strategic concept is not shaken further." He added that this "credibility" had been weakened by "theoreticans" seeking "an alternative to the strategy of the deterrent." Strauss was convinced that any self-imposed limitation on the use of nuclear weapons would increase the danger of war.[15] Germany, however, remained firmly wedded to the alliance, despite friction with the United States over the direction of NATO strategy. The Adenauer government was committed totally to the military integration of the alliance and resisted a display of Gaullist antipathy towards the United States. In fact, Germany was the only European member to substantially increase the conventional capability of its armed forces. The German government extended the period of conscription to eighteen months and increased the manpower goal of the Bundeswehr from 350,000 to 500,000 men as its contribution to NATO solidarity during the 1961 Berlin Crisis. Finally, the Federal Republic's defense budget rose from 10 billion DM in 1960 to 14.98 DM in 1962.

France proved to be an intractable problem for the Kennedy Administration. During his visit to Paris in June 1961, President Kennedy learned first hand the depth of de Gaulle's disenchantment with the existing political arrangements within NATO. In brief, the French president firmly believed that the loss of the America's nuclear monopoly had significantly reduced the value of America's guarantee to defend Europe. While de Gaulle emphasized the need to "reform" NATO, he assured Kennedy that France would do nothing to undermine the unity of the alliance while Berlin remained a problem. Kennedy assured de Gaulle that if the Soviet Union threatened to overrun Western Europe, the United States was prepared to respond with nuclear weapons.

De Gaulle doubted that and said, in his judgment, the United States would use nuclear weapons only when it's own territory was directly threatened; and why not — this is the way all states behaved. De Gaulle said he would take the president at his word, but could anyone really be certain? During their final conversation, Kennedy proposed that they consider establishing a mechanism of consultation, both military and political, between France, Britain and the United States. De Gaulle agreed, suggesting that the matter might be discussed after the German elections in the fall. Kennedy also suggested that the two leaders should meet frequently, and that the study of a tripartite strategy should be conducted by military experts of three nations and common positions be prepared "whenever possible."[16] The study, however, was never conducted.

In August de Gaulle sent a secret letter to Kennedy in which the French president set forth his concerns about the Berlin situation, raised the issue of a tripartite organization, and presented his rationale for building a *force de frappe*. Kennedy did not respond immediately. The American president gave a sense of his perspective in his September address on disarmament to the U.N. General Assembly, in which he assigned the highest priority to the need to prevent the proliferation of nuclear weapons. Kennedy did not formally answer de Gaulle's August letter until 31 December. Kennedy discussed at length the need for negotiations with the Soviets on Berlin and the Franco-American dispute on nuclear policy. De Gaulle sent a second letter to Kennedy on January 9, 1962, and once again he expressed his hostility towards any negotiations with Moscow on a Berlin settlement and the reasons he intended to continue with France's nuclear development. Kennedy also ignored the second letter.

The Kennedy Administration moved forcefully during the spring of 1962 to define the two main tracks of its policy towards Europe: first, to bolster European confidence that the U.S. nuclear commitment to NATO was secure, and second, to oppose a French national deterrent. In January 1962 Secretary of Defense McNamara stated that the United States "should not preclude the use of tactical nuclear weapons" in a limited war but the decision to use these weapons "should not be forced upon us simply because we have no other means to cope with them."[17]

Kennedy told Stewart Alsop in March that if the Soviets attacked Western Europe, the U.S. "must be prepared to use nuclear weapons at the start, come what may...."[18] The White House Press Office subsequently denied that the president's remarks represented a change in U.S. policy. The interview outraged Khrushchev, and he vented his anger to Pierre Salinger, who was in Moscow at the Soviet premier's invitation. "This warmonger Alsop—is he now your Secretary of State? Not even Dulles would have made the statement your President made. He now forces us to reappraise our own situation."[19] Khrushchev subsequently used Kennedy's comments for his own propaganda advantage. "...the President of the U.S.A. himself, Mr. Kennedy has said that in certain circumstances the U.S.A. may be the first to take the initiative and start a nuclear war against our country. This we must constantly remember comrades. This has been said by the American President...." declared Mr. Khrushchev in Rumania in June 1962. "Ponder these words," he told the Moscow Peace Congress a month later. "They represent not only a threat of thermo-nuclear war but also the imposition of a sinister competition as to who will be the first to unleash a war; they are thus, as it were, prompting other countries, 'to hurry up in order to forestall the enemy.' And where can that lead to? That is clear to everyone—to catastrophic consequences."[20]

President Kennedy's comments in March served to set the stage for Secretary of Defense McNamara's attendance at the Athens meeting of NATO defense ministers in May. The primary purpose of McNamara's remarks to the North Atlantic Council was to present the reasons that national nuclear forces in Europe were injurious to European security. He urged his opposite numbers to solicit a wide range of views from their respective military staffs and to speak for themselves on matters of strategy without being burdened by the orthodoxy of the past. Moreover, he won agreement for the establishment of a Nuclear Planning Group within NATO to foster greater collaboration on nuclear matters among the member states.[21]

Mr. McNamara reaffirmed the key points of his Athens presentation during his commencement address in June to the graduates of the University of Michigan. Without referring to the *force de frappe* by name, McNamara made clear that the small size and vulnerability of such forces would offer an inviting target for a preemptive attack by an aggressor. "In the event of war, the use of such a force against the cities of a major nuclear power would be tantamount to suicide, whereas its employment against significant military targets would have a negligible effect on the outcome of the conflict." Furthermore, "the creation of a single additional national nuclear force encourages the proliferation of nuclear power with all of its attendant dangers."[22]

While McNamara was speaking in Athens, President Kennedy was expressing his confidence in the adequacy of existing nuclear plans to protect Europe and condemning the *force de frappe*. "Once you begin, nation after nation, beginning to develop its own deterrent, or rather feeling it's necessary as an element of its independence to develop its own deterrent, it seems to me you are moving into an increasingly dangerous situation."[23] The president was even more explicit in June, declaring that national nuclear deterrents were "inimical to the community interest of the Atlantic Alliance...."[24] There was, however, an important element of inconsistency in the Kennedy Administration's attitude towards nuclear proliferation. Just before the Ann Arbor address, it became known that the U.S. government was authorizing the Boeing Aircraft Company to sell France a dozen KC-135 jet tanker planes, to be used to refuel the Mirage IV bombers of the *force de frappe.* This was a vital contribution, since France did not have other tanker planes immediately available to extend the short range of the Mirage IVs so that they would be capable of reaching Soviet targets and returning.

President Kennedy and Prime Minister Macmillan sent a proposed draft of a Limited Test Ban Treaty to Khrushchev on August 27, 1962. The Chinese Communists subsequently revealed that two days earlier, Khrushchev had informed Beijing that Secretary of State Rusk had "proposed an agreement stipulating that, first, the nuclear powers should undertake to refrain from transferring nuclear weapons and technical information concerning their manufacture to non-nuclear countries, and that, secondly, the countries not in possession of nuclear weapons should undertake to refrain from manufacturing them, from seeking them from the nuclear powers or from accepting technical information concerning their manufacture." To Beijing's great ire, Khrushchev "gave an affirmative reply" to this proposal, and on three occasions attempted to persuade the Chinese to terminate their nuclear development program.[25] It took the Cuban missile crisis to persuade both superpowers of the value of collaborating to prohibit French and Chinese membership in the nuclear club. Khrushchev agreed to remove the Soviet missiles from Cuba on October 28, 1962. In his letter to Kennedy, Khrushchev added that the Soviet Union wished "to continue to exchange opinions on the proliferation of atomic and thermonuclear weapons, on general disarmament and on other questions relating to the relaxation of international tensions." In his response of the same date, Mr. Kennedy stated "we should give priority to questions relating to the proliferation of nuclear weapons, on earth and in outer space, and to the great effort for the nuclear test ban."[26] The Skybolt controversy, which broke open shortly after the crisis, gave a new sense of urgency to the issue.

Skybolt and the MLF Controversy

British Prime Minister Harold Macmillan journeyed to Camp David in March 1960 with a serious strategic problem in hand. Britain had just cancelled its Blue Streak program, a liquid-fueled MRBM, because of its cost and vulnerability to attack. Moreover, the V-bombers of the Royal Air Force required immediate modernization. The Skybolt air-launched ballistic missile, then under development by the U.S., offered an obvious solution to the British dilemma. President Eisenhower offered to continue the development of Skybolt and make it available to the British. Macmillan offered the United States a base for its Polaris submarines at Holy Loch, Scotland. The two transactions were not explicitly linked, but Macmillan considered Skybolt to be the *quid pro quo* for the base privileges at Holy Loch.[27]

Skybolt was an extremely complex system, and the program encountered serious difficulties with the missile's guidance package. The astro-inertial instrument system fell short of a design goal by a factor of 15 and the inertial platform control system by a factor of 6.[28] The severity of these problems prompted Eisenhower's Secretary of Defense, Thomas Gates, to cut the Skybolt program from his administration's final defense budget. McNamara restored the program for purely political reasons. The new Secretary of Defense had his budgetary sights on eliminating the B-70 bomber, another priority program of the Air Force. McNamara believed he couldn't abolish both weapons simultaneously, so he held out Skybolt with one hand, as he prepared to take away the B-70 bomber with the other. McNamara nevertheless informed President Kennedy and Secretary of State Rusk, early in November, that he intended to terminate the Skybolt program.

News of the decision leaked to the press on 7 December, four days prior to McNamara's arrival in London to discuss the matter with Mr. Peter Thorneycroft, the British Minister of Defense. Upon his arrival at Gatwick Airport, McNamara read a prepared statement to the British press.

> Mr. Thorneycroft and I will have a full discussion.... One of the things we are going to talk about ... is the Skybolt program....
> In Washington ... we are taking a very hard look at all of our programs. This includes Skybolt ... it is a very expensive program and technically extremely complex. It is no secret that all five flight tests attempted so far have failed and program costs have climbed sharply.[29]

When the papers hit the street, Whitehall was outraged by McNamara's cavalier attitude. Predictably, the meeting between the men was strained. Thorneycroft expected McNamara to offer Polaris as a substitute for Skybolt, and McNamara expected Thorneycroft to accede gracefully to the demise of Skybolt and ask for Polaris himself. Richard Neustadt later suggested in a report to the president that the storm was simply caused "by successive failures on the part of busy persons to perceive and make allowance for the needs and wants of others."[30]

The imbroglio was finally settled after four days of discussions between Kennedy and Macmillan in Nassau in December. The British refused to accept either joint development of Skybolt or to take the Hound Dog, a defense suppression missile, as a substitute for Skybolt. Macmillan would settle for nothing less than Polaris. The final agreement stipulated that the United States would provide the missile while Britain would manufacture the warheads and the submarines. The British Polaris submarines, along with the V-bombers, would be targeted according to a joint Anglo-American plan. Britain also pledged to make these forces available for inclusion in a NATO multilateral nuclear force that would include at least an equal number of U.S. strategic weapon systems. Macmillan, however, demanded an escape clause. Accordingly, the agreement specified that the British nuclear contingent would be committed to the defense of the Western Alliance "in all circumstances except where HMG [Her Majesty's Government] may decide that supreme national interests are at stake...."[31]

Both Kennedy and Macmillan realized that the exclusion of France from this agreement would have a devastating effect on the unity of the North Atlantic Alliance. Consequently, they invited France to accept Polaris on the same terms at Britain. Unfortunately, the news of the offer reached the media before it was to be formally presented to President de Gaulle. The incident undoubtedly heightened his suspicions and served to reinforce his displeasure with the behavior of the British and Americans. Ambassador Charles Bohlen, who was present at the Nassau talks, returned immediately to Paris with instructions to explain the agreement to President de Gaulle. Ambassador Bohlen told de Gaulle on January 5, 1963, that all possibilities for multilateral control arrangements were open to discussion. The general displayed no enthusiasm for the Nassau agreement; he showed no acrimony towards it either. Bohlen left the audience thinking that de Gaulle would explore the negotiating implications in due course. Four days later, Undersecretary of State George Ball met with French Foreign Minister Couve de Murville enroute to Bonn to reassure the German government.[32]

De Gaulle gave his answer to London and Washington in a news conference on January 14, 1963. France, he announced, would veto Britain's entry into the Common Market, conclude a treaty of cooperation with the Federal Republic and reject the multilateral force concept spelled out in Nassau. The reason, he explained, was that this "multilateral force necessarily entails a web of liaisons, transmissions and interferences within itself and on the outside a ring of obligations such that, if an integral part was suddenly snatched from it, there would be a strong risk of paralyzing it just at the moment, perhaps, when it should act. In sum, we will adhere to the decisions we have made; to construct and, if necessary, to employ our atomic force ourselves."[33]

During the next two years, the United States and its European allies, to the exclusion of France, devoted an inordinate amount of time and effort to make the MLF a reality. Ambassador Livingston Merchant barnstormed Europe to gain support for President Kennedy's idea of a mixed-manned fleet of twenty-five surface ships armed with Polaris A-3 missiles, capable of a range of 2,500 miles.[34] A working group, composed of the NATO ambassadors of eight interested countries, began technical discussions on the MLF in Paris. These talks continued throughout 1964.

The West Germans were the most enthusiastic supporters of the MLF, and Bonn offered to underwrite 40 percent of its costs. The reason for its support was quite straightforward: The MLF would bring Germany directly into the business of strategic nuclear weapons in a way that would minimize the political risks and costs. The British were skeptical about the entire enterprise and reluctant to take any steps that would delimit their own nuclear capabilities and impinge upon their "special relationship" with the United States. Nevertheless, they gave diplomatic support to the idea. Italy endorsed the concept, but there was uncertainty within the alliance about the degree of support, given the ruling Christian Democrats' courtship of the Italian Left.[35]

De Gaulle's 14 January announcement was followed in short order by the consummation of a Franco-German treaty that included a clause providing for mutual military consultations. The Soviet government sent notes to Paris and Bonn on 5 February and warned publicly of "immediately necessary measures" should West Germany acquire access to nuclear weapons "directly or indirectly."[36] At the same time, Soviet representatives at the International Atomic Energy Agency in Vienna expressed a willingness "to help prevent the use for military purposes of nuclear reactors given to underdeveloped countries."[37]

The night after the Nassau Agreement was signed, one of President Kennedy's close aides ventured the observation that the entire MLF was a misbegotten idea. "A multi-national ship? We have trouble enough in our own Navy running a ship where everybody in the crew speaks English." "Who cares?" the president responded:

> It may take them a few years to straighten out the language problem, and longer than that to straighten out the other problems. But in the meantime Macmillan is happy as a clam. He's going home to England with a nuclear missile ship. Maybe there'll never be such a ship and maybe nothing really happened here today, but that's beside the point. The point is that we got Macmillan off the hook.[38]

The Sino-Soviet Split

Any effort to pin down exactly when the Sino-Soviet controversy began is laced with uncertainty. A historian might point to Stalin's acquiescence of Chiang K'ai-shek's suppression of the Communists in the Kuomintang during the Canton uprising in 1927. A political scientist, on the other hand, would typically turn to the Twentieth Party Congress in his analysis of the controversy. A strategist, however, would pay particular attention to the events surrounding the October 1957 conclave of ruling Communist Parties held in Moscow.

If one were to consider the final declaration alone, the political health of the Sino-Soviet alliance was excellent. Moscow and Beijing had found common ground on which to denounce the Yugoslav heresy. In the words of the declaration, "the main danger at the present is revisionism or, in other words, right-wing opportunism, which as a manifestation of bourgeois ideology paralyzes the revolutionary energy of the working class and demands the preservation or restoration of capitalism."[39] However, Mao was as concerned with the military aspects of the alliance as he was with its political strength. In his talks with the Soviets, Mao wanted to determine when and how the Soviet nuclear deterrent would be invoked to cover military moves against the offshore islands of Quemoy and Matsu and whether the Soviets would aid China's acquisition of an atomic bomb. According to the Chinese, both nations concluded an agreement on October 15, 1957, in which the Soviets agreed to provide "new technology for national defense."[40] Mao and his Defense Minister, P'eng Teh-huai, were ebullient. Speaking to a group of Chinese students at Moscow State University on 17 November, Mao declared, "At present, it is not the West wind which is prevailing over the East wind, but the East wind prevailing over the West wind." The next day, he told the members of the Supreme Soviet that "all self-styled powerful reactionaries" were "paper tigers."[41]

Early the next summer, Ambassador P.F. Yudin approached the Chinese with an official Soviet request to build a radio relay station in China to communicate with Soviet submarines on patrol in the Pacific as well as to have port privileges for the same boats.[42] The Chinese reaction, according to Khrushchev, was "stormy and irate." Khrushchev and Malinovskiy left Moscow secretly on 31 July for three days of consultations with Mao and compatriots. The Chinese once again refused to honor the Soviet request, although Mao reassured the Soviet delegation that should war come the Socialist Camp would triumph by numbers alone. Khrushchev left Beijing "wondering how our ally . . . could have such a childish outlook on the problem of war."[43]

The Communist Chinese artillery bombardment of the Nationalist garrisons on Quemoy and Matsu began on August 23, 1958. Khrushchev's threat to President Eisenhower that "an attack on the PRC . . . is an attack on the Soviet Union" came only after the risk of escalation had passed. Years later, the Chinese bitterly recounted: "It was only when they [the Soviets] were clear that this was the situation [that there was no possibility that a nuclear war would break out] that the Soviet leaders expressed this support for China."[44] With the Taiwan Straits Crisis in mind, and a Soviet-American summit in the offing, Khrushchev tore up the nuclear assistance agreement with China on June 20, 1959.

The Sino-Soviet dispute intensified the following year. On April 16, 1960, the Beijing daily, *Red Flag*, published an article entitled "Long Live Leninism," rumored to have been written by Mao. This piece was the opening shot in the public war of words between China and the Soviets. The article dismissed Khrushchev's dictum of the non-inevitability of war and stated that "until the imperialist system and the exploitive class come to an end, wars of one kind or another will always occur." The most contentious assertion, however, was the claim that "on the debris of a dead imperialism, the victorious people would create very swiftly a civilization thousands of times higher than the capitalist system and a truly beautiful future for themselves."[45]

The Soviet response came the following week in a speech by veteran Finnish Communist and Praesidium member Otto Kuusinen. Kuusinen chided those who "repeat the old truth that imperialism is aggressive." His key point, however, was that "new types of weapons are able, not only to bring about a radical change in the art of war, but also to influence politics." To prove the proposition, he unearthed a previously unknown anecdote. According to Lenin's wife, Krupskaya, the former Bolshevik leader foresaw "the time ... when war will become so destructive as to be impossible."[46]

In early June, Chinese delegates at the World Federation of Trade Unions meeting in Beijing criticized the Soviet policy line and actively lobbied among delegates against the Kremlin. In the words of one Chinese delegate, "If we only talk about the possibility of stopping the imperialists from launching a world war..., and are not on the alert against the military adventures of the war mongers, we will only lull ourselves and the people."[47] Khrushchev was outraged and saw the Chinese behavior as an impermissible breach of discipline. The Soviet counterattack came at the end of the month, and the occasion was the Congress of the Rumanian Communist Party. At that meeting, attended by representatives of some fifty parties, the Soviets circulated a long Party letter, sharply critical of the Chinese positions, accusing the Chinese of "disloyal and uncomradely" behavior, and hinting clearly that the U.S.S.R. would reduce its aid to China unless the Chinese Communist Party backed down. Bitter exchanges took place, Khrushchev attacking Mao personally for being as vain and isolated from reality as was Stalin, the Chinese attacking Khrushchev for having "betrayed" Marx, Lenin, and Stalin. In the end, a thin and ambiguous communique was composed which resolved nothing but did announce that another, larger conference would be held in Moscow in the fall.[48]

Khrushchev made good on his threat, and 1,390 Soviet specialists left China by the end of August. The Soviets also tore up 343 contracts and supplementary agreements and scrapped 257 scientific and technical projects. A Chinese delegation arrived in Moscow in mid–September for five days of consultations, but nothing was settled. At the end of the month, twenty-six parties assembled to prepare the "manifesto" for the conference of Eighty-One Communist and Workers' Parties scheduled to open in early November. Nearly 165 pages of amendments were added to the Soviet draft. The conference adjourned abruptly on 24 November because of seemingly intractable differences between the Soviet and Chinese parties. It was not until 1 December that Party Secretary Mikhail Suslov announced that complete agreement between the two sides had been reached.[49]

A central point of contention during the previous nine months involved the question of war and peace. The Soviet view was that war is a political act, waged for political ends. Nuclear war, however, would be senseless in view of its consequences, and thus would not serve the intended political goals. The Chinese held fast to the idea that every war is a continuation of politics, although they admitted that improvements in the "superiority" of the Socialist Camp served to deter the outbreak of nuclear war. The Chinese contended that a number of important opportunities existed to wage wars of national liberation and revolutionary civil war. Moreover, they accused the Soviets of betraying the revolutionary struggle by their support of peaceful coexistence and assertion that local wars can rapidly escalate into world wars when the superpowers are drawn into the fighting. The November conference failed to reconcile Sino-Soviet differences on this issue as well as on all of the others. The final statement was a complex and tortured document. There was no evidence of compromise, but rather an agreement to disagree. For example, strong emphasis was placed, in Soviet terms, on the horrific consequences of nuclear war. The Chinese point that the nature of imperialism has not changed was affirmed, but with the Soviet caveat that world war is not inevitable.

The Kennedy Administration completely misread Khrushchev's January 1961 report on the conference and his statement in support of wars of national liberation. Khrushchev's speech served to confirm Kennedy's worst fears about Soviet intentions, and it became a prime justification for the military initiatives that the Kennedy Administration was about to introduce. Early in his term of office, Kennedy believed that a split between the two Communist giants was not something America ought to "look forward to with comfort." "It could bring us harm," Kennedy told an off-the-record briefing of journalists at the State Department, "if Khrushchev has to prove his revolutionary intensity."[50] Khrushchev's condemnation of Albania at the Twenty-First Party Congress and Zhou En-lai's abrupt departure in protest did not seem to move the president to reexamine his perception of a monolithic Sino-Soviet Bloc. Allen Dulles cautioned the National Security Council on November 15, 1961, that it should not be assumed that the Chinese setbacks as well as the ideological rift were such that the Soviets and Chinese would not be able nor willing to engage jointly any nation which threatened Communist interests.[51] A significant shift in President Kennedy's attitude towards the Sino-Soviet dispute did not begin to occur until after the Cuban missile crisis.

On October 22, 1962, President Kennedy declared a "quarantine" of all Soviet "offensive weapons" entering Cuba. Two days earlier, the Chinese People's Liberation Army had attacked in force India's northeast frontier area and the region of Ladakh. Within a month, Chinese forces stood at the foothills of Assam and little stood between them and Calcutta.[52] Soviet support of the Indians angered the Chinese and added to the fury of their condemnation of Khrushchev's behavior during the Cuban crisis. *Peoples Daily* claimed on 31 December that "a compromise of this sort can only be regarded as 100 percent appeasement, a 'Munich' pure and simple...." According to *Red Flag* on 4 January, "A political leader must know how to distinguish compromises that are permissible from those compromises that are impermissible and are an expression of treachery...." *Pravda* reacted with a biting editorial attack on January 7, 1963, against "leftist phrasemongers."

> The "paper tiger" definition of imperialism speaks only of its weaknesses.... What we need are not paper definitions, ... but a genuine analysis.... Marxism-Leninism teaches us to approach the enemy with a sober estimate of prospects and actual forces.... The world Communist movement is well aware that imperialism is on the decline..., but it is also aware that it has atomic fangs, to which it may resort....[53]

In his State of the Union address on January 14, 1963, President Kennedy acknowledged that the "winds of change appear to be blowing more strongly than ever in the world of communism as well as ours." Although he anticipated no spectacular reversals in Communist methods or goals, the president sought an accommodation with the Soviets.

> ...if all these trends and developments can persuade the Soviet Union to walk the path of peace, let them know that all free nations will journey with her.[54]

The Nuclear Test Ban Negotiations

On December 19, 1962, Khrushchev wrote to Kennedy and stated that the time had come "to put a stop to nuclear tests once and for all, to make an end to them."[55] The United States and the Soviet Union began separate talks on disarmament the next month in New York. Kennedy made clear, at a White House review of the U.S. negotiating position on 22 January, that the Chinese nuclear program was the driving force behind his quest for a test ban treaty. One important consideration was the power that the Chinese would have with nuclear weapons and how they would use that power. If a test ban treaty could lessen that prospect, the president believed that the U.S. should think twice before turning it down. He suspected that the Soviets were think-ing much the same about it. He said that a test ban that affected only the Russians and the United States would have only limited value but, if there was a chance it could affect the Chinese, it would be worth very much indeed. In this sense, it was more important to the world situa-tion than it had been a year or two ago. He added that the CIA agreed with this assessment.[56] By the end of the month, however, it became clear that neither side was willing to compromise on verification ar-rangements for a comprehensive test ban. The talks broke down, and the U.S. prepared to resume testing.

The president met with his principal advisors on 1 February to discuss the U.S. approach once negotiations resumed. The president stated that a ratification fight in the Senate would be pointless if it weren't for stopping China's nuclear weapons program. He directed his advisors to frame the U.S. position on inspections on the assump-tion that the U.S.S.R. would cheat, and he ordered them to work out the relative advantages by a comparison of what the Soviets might gain by clandestine underground testing under a comprehensive treaty with the advantages the treaty might bring in preventing the spread of nuclear weapons particularly to China.[57]

The negotiations reopened in New York and once again became mired in the inspection issue, the U.S. holding out for seven on-site inspections while the Soviets held firm to two or three. As the deadlock continued, the United States prepared to resume testing.[58] There was a break in the stalemate on 5 April, when the Soviet Union agreed to the United States proposal for a direct communications link, the "hot line," between Washington and Moscow, to reduce the threat of ac-cidental war. The test ban negotiations were still deadlocked. Kennedy and Macmillan sent a joint message to Khrushchev on 31 May. The Soviet premier replied on 8 June and agreed to reconvene the negotia-tions in Moscow on 15 July. Two days later, President Kennedy de-livered a major foreign policy address at American University.

> Let us focus instead on a more practical, more attainable peace, based not on a sudden revolution in human nature but on a gradual evolution in human institutions — on a series of concrete actions and effective agreements which are in the interest of all concerned.[59]

On July 2, 1963, in a speech in East Berlin, Khrushchev expressed his readiness to conclude an agreement on the cessation of nuclear tests in the atmosphere, in outer space, and underwater. Khrushchev added one major complication, however: a proposal for a non-aggression pact between NATO and the United States. Although this issue caused concern in the administration because of French and German opposition, it did not present a stumbling block during the negotiations.

President Kennedy selected W. Averell Harriman to head the U.S. delegation to the Moscow test ban negotiations. Harriman's instructions were finalized at a meeting in the White House on 9 July. The president asked Mr. Harriman whether anything could be done to bring the Chinese into line. Mr. Harriman responded that it was doubtful that the Soviets would even discuss this problem.[60] Harriman and his deputy, Dr. Carl Kaysen, met privately with the president shortly before their departure. Mr. Harriman asked the president whether he would agree to let him talk to Khrushchev about Communist China "and the possibility of our cooperation with the Soviet Union when Red China got [its] nuclear capability." The president said, "By all means," but Harriman added that he would need an enticement to sweeten the offer. Kennedy enquired what this might be, and Harriman stated, "Throw in the MLF." According to Mr. Harriman's recollection, the president waved his hand and said "Of course — it would be great to get rid of that!"[61] Schlesinger's account adds the following presidential comment to the conversation: "I have some cash in the bank in West Germany and am prepared to draw on it if you think I should."[62]

The Sino-Soviet reconciliation talks, agreed to in March, opened in Moscow on 5 July; ten days later, the final round of the test ban negotiations began. The Soviet draft treaty was composed of two operative paragraphs. The first prohibited nuclear testing in the atmosphere, outer space and underwater. The second paragraph stated that the agreement would enter into force immediately on signature by the Soviet Union, Great Britain, the United States and France. Both Harriman and his British counterpart, Lord Hailsham, protested the inclusion of France, although they acknowledged that France's ultimate adherence to the treaty was important. The discussion of France permitted Harriman to raise the question of China. Khrushchev did not appear disturbed by the prospect and assured Harriman that it would be "a long time" before China possessed a nuclear arsenal comparable to the U.S. and the Soviet Union.[63]

Kennedy replied to Harriman's report of the first negotiating session on the same day:

> Your report is encouraging on limited test ban. You are right to keep French out of initial treaty, though I continue to be prepared

to work on French if Soviets will work on Chinese, and you should make this clear as occasion offers. I remain convinced that Chinese problem is more serious than Khrushchev suggests and believe you should press question with him in private meeting.... I agree that large stockpiles are characteristic of U.S. and U.S.S.R. only but consider that relatively small forces in hands of people like Chicoms could be very dangerous to us all. You should try to elicit K's view of means of limiting or preventing Chinese nuclear development and his willingness either to take Soviet action or to accept U.S. action aimed in this direction.[64]

The last sentence of the cable sounded suspiciously like an invitation to a preemptive attack against the Chinese nuclear facilities near Lake Lop Nor in Xinjiang Province.

The Sino-Soviet negotiations broke off on July 20, 1963. The final communique stated that "both sides set forth their views and positions on a whole series of important questions of principle affecting current changes in the world situation, the international Communist movement and Soviet-Chinese relations." The talks recessed at the request of the Chinese.[65]

Harriman did not have another opportunity to discuss China with Khrushchev until after the treaty was initialed on July 25, 1963. When the opportunity came, Khrushchev was prickly and refused to discuss China with a capitalist. Harriman persisted and asked, "Suppose we can get France to sign the treaty? Can you deliver China?" Khrushchev told Harriman that China was America's problem. Harriman tried again: "Suppose their rockets are targeted against you?" Khrushchev refused to answer.[66]

Kennedy addressed the American people on July 26, 1963. "The treaty is not the millenium," he told his audience. "It will not resolve all conflicts, or cause the Communists to forego their ambitions, or eliminate the dangers of war." But the treaty was, in his words, "a shaft of light cut into the darkness" and "a step towards reduced world tension and broader areas of agreement."[67] The president referred to the treaty as "an important opening wedge in our effort to 'get the genie back in the bottle.'"[68] The treaty was formally signed in Moscow on August 5, 1963, by Secretary of State Rusk, Foreign Minister Gromyko, and Foreign Minister Lord Home.

The Aftermath

President Kennedy's concern about China and France persisted even after the negotiations. On July 30, 1963, Mr. Kennedy ordered a meeting of his National Security Council for the following day to discuss Chinese political intentions. CIA Director John McCone responded with a Special National Intelligence Estimate entitled *Possibilities of Greater Militancy by the Chinese Communists.* The purpose of the estimate was "to consider the possibility of more asser- tive Chinese Communist actions in the near future, arising from the coincidence of deepening Sino-Soviet disputes and recent Soviet nego- tiations with the West." The U.S. Intelligence Board concluded that "we do not believe that they [the Chinese] will act recklessly or run very great risks, such as a renewal of the Korean War or even a major inva- sion deep into India." "New pressures on the Indian border and in Laos" were considered the "most likely" initiatives by Beijing. "Ser- ious" clashes along the Sino-Soviet border "would tend to reduce the likelihood of Chinese Communist moves against its other borders."[69]

The president was still wary. He told reporters at a news con- ference on 1 August that China presented the United States with a "menacing situation." The introduction of nuclear weapons in China would create "potentially a more dangerous situation than any we faced since the end of the Second World War...." The president stated that "we would like to take some steps now which would lessen that prospect that a future president might have to deal with." The test ban treaty, despite its limitations, was a step in the right direction.[70] Kennedy then declared that France was a nuclear power "in terms of the Atomic Energy Act." He made clear, however, that future assis- tance would depend not only on France's meeting the requirements of the McMahon Act but also on her political cooperation with NATO. In the president's words, assistance depended on "the organization of the defense of the West, and what role France sees for herself, and sees for us, and what kind of a cooperative effort for France and the United States and Britain and other members of NATO...."[71]

De Gaulle rejected Kennedy's offer on 4 August. He stressed in- stead his intention to continue French nuclear tests and to make no ar- rangements that would jeopardize the independence of France. China condemned the Limited Test Ban Treaty as a "fraud" intended to pre- vent Chinese Communists "from increasing their defense capability." Chinese animus was intense towards Moscow. "The indisputable facts prove that the policy pursued by the Soviet Government is one of ally- ing with the forces of war to oppose the forces of peace, allying with imperialism to oppose socialism, allying with the United States to op- pose China, and allying with the reactionaries of all countries to op- pose the people of the world."[72] The Soviet response was equally blunt:

The point is: whose judgments on these matters carry weight, and whose smack of idle chatter.... Has anyone asked the Chinese that are being doomed to death whether they want to serve as fuel in the furnace of a missile nuclear war? Did they authorize the CPR leadership to sign their death certificates in advance.[73]

China now began to accelerate its development of an atomic bomb. "Soviet protection is worth nothing to us," remarked Chinese Foreign Minister Ch'en I in December. "No outsiders can give us protection, in fact, because they always attach conditions and want to control us."[74] Several days later, Secretary Rusk was reported to have "virtually pleaded" with the members of the North Atlantic Council to help Khrushchev in his struggle with China. It was necessary, he allegedly said, to go easy on Khrushchev so that the radicals in Beijing would reap no rewards for their militancy elsewhere.[75] On January 27, 1964, France announced the opening of diplomatic relations with China. Khrushchev's political capital at home was virtually exhausted. Even detente could not help him. On October 14, 1964, the Central Committee ousted Khrushchev from power. Forty-eight hours later, China detonated its first atomic bomb.[76]

Chapter 5

Deterrence in Practice: Cuba 1962

The whole area of war is being transformed into mere prudence, with the primary aim of preventing the uncertain balance from shifting suddenly to disadvantage and half-war from developing into total war.

Clausewitz

A Smell of Burning in the Air
N.S. Khrushchev

A Chronology of the Crisis

The Cuban missile crisis actually began during the summer of 1962. U.S. intelligence noted a sudden rise in July of Soviet military aid to Castro as ship arrivals to Cuban ports increased dramatically. An average of fifteen Soviet dry cargo ships per month arrived in Cuba during the first half of 1962. The number jumped to thirty-seven in August. Only one Soviet passenger ship arrived in Cuba during the first six months of 1962. Four arrived in July and six arrived in August. At the same time, the CIA reception center in Miami began to receive a growing number of refugee reports of alleged missile activity on the island. Field agents began to report that some of the Soviet ships were unloaded in Mariel at night under rigid security with all Cubans being barred from the immediate vicinity.[1] These persistent reports were consistently discounted by intelligence analysts at CIA, except for the agency's director, John McCone, because so risky a gamble with the peace of the world seemed incredible.[2]

The upsurge in Soviet arms deliveries prompted the president to issue National Security Action Memorandum No. 181 on August 23, 1962. Three of the five declassified requirements are particularly noteworthy. The president directed the Defense Department to determine what action could be taken to get the Jupiter missiles out of

111

Turkey. The NSC staff was instructed to prepare an analysis of the "probable military, political and psychological impact of the establishment in Cuba of either surface-to-air missiles or surface-to-surface missiles which could reach the U.S." Finally, the Defense Department was also tasked to prepare a study "of the various military alternatives which might be adopted in executing a decision to eliminate any installations in Cuba capable of launching nuclear attack on the U.S. What would be the pros and cons, for example, of a pinpoint attack, general counterforce attack, and outright invasion?"[3]

On 29 August a SAC U-2 reconnaissance plane photographed eight SA-2 antiaircraft batteries in western Cuba along with several cruise missile installations for coastal defense. Inclement weather and heavy cloud cover hampered aerial reconnaissance during the entire month of September and into the beginning of October. This absence of photographic intelligence coincided with Khrushchev's campaign to divert American attention from Cuba and get on with the business of installing surface-to-surface missiles. On 4 September Soviet Ambassador Anatoli Dobrynin met with Robert Kennedy to transmit a personal message from Khrushchev. Dobrynin told the attorney general that he was instructed by Khrushchev to assure President Kennedy that the Soviet Union had no intention of deploying land-based missiles or offensive weapons in Cuba. Further, Dobrynin told Kennedy that Khrushchev would do nothing to upset bilateral relations during this period prior to the congressional elections.[4] The president released a statement the same afternoon that discussed the recent Soviet arms shipments to Cuba and denied that it provided any offensive capability against the United States. However, the president hastened to add that the U.S. would use "whatever may be necessary" to prevent aggression from Cuba.

Two days later, Dobrynin requested an urgent meeting with Theodore Sorenson, the president's special counsel. At the meeting he delivered a second personal message from Mr. Khrushchev to President Kennedy:

> Nothing will be undertaken before the American Congressional elections that could complicate the international situation or aggravate the tension in relations between our two countries.... The Chairman does not wish to be involved in your internal affairs.[5]

Dobrynin's efforts were complemented by Georgi Bolshakov, a Soviet official who carried Khrushchev's personal messages to the White House the year before during the Berlin crisis. This time he relayed a message from Khrushchev and Anastas Mikoyan to various members of the administration: "No missiles capable of reaching the United States would be placed in Cuba."[6] These private assurances were balanced by a veiled warning issued in Moscow on 13 September:

> The Government of the Soviet Union authorized TASS to state there is no need for the Soviet Union to shift its weapons for the repulsion of aggression, for a retaliatory blow, to any other country, for instance Cuba. Our nuclear weapons are so powerful in their explosive force and the Soviet Union has so powerful rockets to carry these nuclear warheads, that there is no need to search for sites for them beyond the boundaries of the Soviet Union.

The statement claimed that the current Soviet arms shipments to Cuba were an "internal affair" and "no business" of the Americans. The statement tersely warned: "Don't butt your noses where you oughtn't."[7]

The U.S. pressed its surveillance of Cuba at the insistence of John McCone. His fears were confirmed on 14 October when a U-2 returned to its base with the first hard evidence that the Soviets were building medium-range missile sites in Cuba. The high-altitude photographs revealed construction near San Cristobal and Sagua la Grandi. Tanker trucks, power and instrument installations, missile guidance stations, and erector launchers were clearly visible. SAC flew twenty U-2 sorties over the island, and low-altitude flights by Air Force RF-4 Phantoms began on the 23rd. The materials provided by Colonel Oleg Penkovskiy supplemented these photographs and allowed the CIA to follow the progress of Soviet missile emplacement by the hour.[8] Nine of the twenty-four SS-4 MRBM sites near San Cristobol and Sagua la Grandi were complete or under construction on 22 October. The MRBM sites were expected to be operational by 28 October, and the twelve IRBM launch points were to be finished by 15 December.[9]

Shortly after the discovery of the missiles, the president established a top-level group of advisors, later formally named the Executive Committee of the National Security Council (EXCOM), to consider and recommend various policy alternatives. By Wednesday, 17 October, the EXCOM discussions had gravitated towards two specific options: the first, a "surgical" air strike to destroy the missile sites as well as the IL-28 medium bombers; the second, a naval blockade while diplomatic pressure was exerted on the Soviets to remove their offensive weapons. On Friday, 19 October, the blockade option appeared to have won out, with the caveat that an air strike would follow if diplomacy failed.

In the midst of these closely held discussions, Andrei Gromyko came to see the president. The visit had been scheduled long before the missiles were discovered. Mr. Khrushchev had instructed Gromyko to tell the president that the only assistance being furnished to Cuba was for "agriculture and land development," plus some defensive arms. Kennedy was astonished and read aloud to Gromyko his September 4 statement to avoid any misunderstanding of the U.S. position on the delivery of offensive arms to Cuba.[10] The U-2 photos were on his desk as he spoke.[11]

At 7:00 p.m. on Monday, October 22, 1962, President Kennedy addressed his fellow countrymen. "Within the past week," Kennedy announced, "unmistakable evidence has established the fact that a series of offensive missile sites is now in preparation [in Cuba]. The purpose of these bases can be none other than to provide a nuclear strike capability against the Western Hemisphere."[12] This "secret, swift and extraordinary" buildup of Soviet offensive weapons had transformed Cuba into an "important strategic base." Kennedy labeled the Soviet decision "a deliberately provocative and unjustified change in the status quo." Speaking with modest historical authority, the president raised the specter of Munich and stated that "aggressive conduct, if allowed to go unchecked and unchallenged, ultimately leads to war." He announced a "strict quarantine on all offensive military equipment under shipment to Cuba," and, he warned Khrushchev,

> It shall be the policy of this Nation to regard any nuclear missile launched from Cuba against any nation in the Western Hemisphere as an attack by the Soviet Union on the United States, requiring the full retaliatory response on the Soviet Union.[13]

No president had ever before presented the Soviets with a choice between war or peace in such unambiguous terms. The following day, the Soviet Union and the Warsaw Pact nations increased the readiness of their armed forces. All leaves and retirements for members of the Soviet Strategic Rocket Forces, Air Defense Forces, and submarine service were cancelled and unspecified measures were announced "to raise the combat readiness and vigilance of all troops."[14]

Secretary Rusk quickly obtained the unanimous support of the Organization of American States for the quarantine on 23 October, and expressions of support were forthcoming from the NATO allies. The United States presented its case to the U.N. Security Council that afternoon. The U.S. demanded the immediate withdrawal of the offensive weapons under international inspection. The Soviets condemned the blockade as an act of piracy and called for its immediate termination. Neither resolution was brought to a vote and the Security Council recessed, helpless to ease the crisis.

During the early morning hours of 24 October, a U.S. naval task force of nineteen war ships, led by the cruiser *Newport News*, formed a picket line five hundred miles from Cuba to intercept twenty-five Russian ships. The carriers *Enterprise* and *Independence* took position near Cuba. Some forty-five ships, 240 aircraft and 30,000 men were directly engaged in the blockade. In addition, 25,000 Marines aboard Navy ships and more than 100,000 Army troops in Florida were ready for an invasion of Cuba. These steps were matched by an awesome display of U.S. strategic nuclear power. Polaris boats left port and moved to their combat stations within range of the Soviet Union. SAC bombers were dispersed for the first time to civilian airfields, and about half these bombers were placed on airborne alert. In concert, these forces were capable of delivering in excess of 3,500 megatons against Soviet targets.[15]

The crisis had now reached the point where public opinion would play an important role in the diplomatic struggle. At the urging of British Prime Minister Harold Macmillan, the president agreed to publicize the U-2 photographs.[16] The opportunity came on 25 October in New York. Ambassador Stevenson unveiled blow-ups of U-2 imagery before the Security Council and challenged Soviet Ambassador Valerian Zorin to acknowledge the existence of the missiles in Cuba. Zorin derisively referred to the photos as "falsified information." Angered, Stevenson told Zorin that he was prepared to wait for his answer "until hell freezes over." Toward evening, the Soviet tanker *Bucharest* approached the blockade line, and the American destroyer USS *Gearing* steamed to meet it. The tanker was soon allowed to continue its voyage to Havana. Khrushchev claimed that the ship had not been stopped. The United States claimed that the captain had acknowledged inspection. Neither side was prepared to back down.

Shortly after 10:00 the next morning, the Navy informed the president and his advisors that two Soviet freighters, the *Gagarin* and the *Komiles*, were approaching the American ships with a submarine escort. Twenty-five minutes later, both ships "stopped dead in the water." "We're eyeball to eyeball, and I think the other fellow just blinked," Dean Rusk remarked with a genuine sense of relief.

Work on the missile sites proceeded apace. On Friday, 26 October, Khrushchev sent a rambling and emotional letter to Kennedy that pleaded for a peaceful resolution of the crisis and hinted that the

Soviets might remove their missiles in exchange for a pledge by the United States not to invade Cuba. In Khrushchev's words,

> If you have not lost your self-control and sensibly conceive what this might lead to, then, Mr. President, we and you ought not to pull on the ends of the rope in which you have tied the knot of war, because the more the two of us pull, the tighter the knot will be tied. And a moment may come when the knot will be tied so tight that even he who tied it will not have the strength to untie it, and then it will be necessary to cut that knot, and what that would mean is not for me to explain to you, because you yourself understand perfectly of what terrible forces our countries dispose. Consequently, if there is no intention to tighten that knot, and thereby to doom the world to the catastrophe of thermonuclear war, then let us not only relax the forces pulling on the ends of the rope, let us take measures to untie that knot. We are ready for this.[17]

The next day Radio Moscow broadcast the text of a second letter from Khrushchev in which the Soviet leader demanded the removal of the fifteen U.S. Jupiter missiles from Turkey in exchange for the Soviet missiles in Cuba.[18] At Robert Kennedy's suggestion, the president answered the first letter and ignored the second and pledged not to invade Cuba if the missiles were removed under U.N. supervision. Meanwhile, preparations were underway for an air strike on Monday, 29 October, against targets in Cuba. Lyndon Johnson jotted down the president's decision this way:

> regarding the peace in the Caribbean —
>   By strike no later than Mon. a.m.
>   Invasion[19]

On Sunday, 28 October, the White House received a message from Khrushchev that the Soviet government agreed to remove the missiles and to a U.N. inspection of the process. No mention was made of the Jupiter missiles in Turkey.[20]

The Unanswered Question

In March 1963, Fidel Castro told a sympathetic reporter, Claude Julien, that certain aspects of the missile crisis remained a "mystery" that might be unraveled by historians in "twenty or thirty years."[21] Even after two decades, the central question about the crisis lacks a satisfactory answer: Why did Khrushchev place the missiles in Cuba in the first place? Khrushchev gave his explanation for the crisis in a report to the Supreme Soviet on December 12, 1962. The premier explained that "this small number of IRBMs" was sent to Cuba at the request of the Cuban government to defend the Castro regime against American attack, and the missiles were removed "to preserve peace."[22] Khrushchev went on to say that "The President declared quite definitely, and this is known to the whole world, that the United States would not attack Cuba and would also restrain its allies from such actions."[23] What Khrushchev failed to mention was that the non-invasion pledge was made contingent upon U.N. verification of the removal. Castro balked, and the U.S. was forced to rely on verification by its own aerial reconnaissance. Khrushchev's memoirs add little to our understanding of the crisis. "Our intention," he wrote, "was to install the missiles not to wage war against the U.S., but to prevent the U.S. from invading Cuba and thus start[ing] a war."[24] Contemporary Soviet explanations hold true to the line established by Khrushchev. For example, the most recent edition of *Istoriya Vneshney Politiki SSSR* explains the deployment of missiles to Cuba this way: "In the Summer of 1962, Cuba appealed to the Soviet government with a request to render supplementary assistance in the connection with the growing threat posed by the U.S.A."[25]

A variety of alternative explanations have been proposed by Western analysts. The mainstream interpretation of Soviet motives during the crisis argues that Khrushchev had been emboldened to challenge the U.S. because he perceived Kennedy to be unwilling to defend America's vital interests. The missiles in Cuba, according to this view, would serve as proof that the Soviet Union could defy the United States and establish an "impregnable" base in Cuba from which to exploit social unrest in Latin America. According to James Reston, Khrushchev studied Kennedy's behavior during the Bay of Pigs and concluded that he was dealing with an inexperienced, young leader. The gamble to put offensive missiles into Cuba was a product of this assumption.[26] John Stoessinger cites Khrushchev's comments to Robert Frost and American businessman William Knox in October 1962 to support the hypothesis that Khrushchev perceived Kennedy to be weak. Frost reported Khrushchev as saying that democracies were "too liberal to fight," and Khrushchev reportedly said to Knox, "How can I deal with a man who is younger than my own son?"[27]

Franklin Reeve later disclosed that Khrushchev never made the remark to Frost. The aged American poet simply substituted the word "liberal" for "young" in recounting an earthy anecdote Khrushchev cited from Gorky's memoirs where Tolstoy described himself as "too weak and too infirm to do it but still having the desire."[28] Khrushchev made his comment to Knox on 24 October at the moment when the quarantine was just taking hold. It's not surprising that he was reaching for even the flimsiest excuses to explain away his troubles.

Other scholars have sought to understand Khrushchev's motives by placing the missile crisis within the broader context of Soviet foreign policy. One of the more elegant hypotheses was crafted by Adam Ulam. The missiles, he argues, were the instrument with which Khrushchev hoped "to solve the most gruelling dilemmas of Soviet foreign policy with ... one bold stroke." Khrushchev planned, according to Ulam, to appear before the U.N. General Assembly in November with an offer to remove the missiles if the United States agreed to a German Peace Treaty with an absolute prohibition of nuclear weapons for Bonn and a nuclear free zone in the Pacific in order to extract a pledge from China not to manufacture nuclear weapons.[29]

The argument that Khrushchev intended to use the missiles in trade for the removal of the Jupiter missiles in Turkey, or even to impose a Berlin settlement, does have its shortcomings.[30] Arnold Horelick argues persuasively that a simple trade-off of bases would have made little sense to the Soviets. It was more likely that the exchange proposal contained in Khrushchev's letter of October 27 was "an improvised or perhaps even a prepared fall-back position to cover unfavorable contingencies, but not the Soviet-preferred culmination of the Cuban venture." Moreover, he maintains that "U.S. strategic superiority also made it too risky for the Soviet Union to play or, under the circumstances, even threaten to play, the Berlin trump card."[31]

If one considers the tenor of Soviet-American relations during the two years leading up to the crisis, then Carl Linden's explanation of the missiles is probably closer to the mark. If the plan had succeeded, he writes, "Khrushchev could have claimed that he had redressed in a single stroke the U.S.S.R.'s strategic inferiority to the United States."[32] A few days after Khrushchev's December 1962 speech to the Supreme Soviet, Kennedy was asked to comment on the speech. The president stated that if the Soviet ploy had succeeded, "it would have politically changed the balance of power. It would have appeared to, and appearances contribute to reality."[33] Kennedy's view was corroborated in large measure by an unlikely source, Fidel Castro. Castro explained, in his interview with Julien, that the proposal to emplace the missiles came from Moscow:

> They explained to us that in accepting them we would be reinforcing the socialist camp the world over, and because we had received

important aid from the socialist camp we estimated that we could not decline. This is why we accepted them. It was not in order to assure own defense, but first of all to reinforce socialism on the international scale. Such is the truth even if other explanations are furnished elsewhere.[34]

In this author's opinion, Khrushchev's plan was a bold gamble to restore some semblance of equality to the strategic balance between the Soviet Union and the United States. For over a year, Kennedy and his Secretary of Defense had flaunted U.S. strategic superiority and relished Khrushchev's discomfort. Khrushchev frankly admitted in his memoirs that he "tried to derive maximum political advantage from the fact we were the first to launch our rockets into space. We wanted to exert pressure on the militarists — and also influence the minds of more reasonable politicians — so that the United States would start treating us better."[35] It took a crisis of dire proportions for both leaders to recognize their mutual responsibilities as well as their mutual security interests.

The limited detente that followed on the heels of the Cuban crisis led to a degree of collaboration unprecedented in the postwar development of Soviet-American relations. However, in the opinion of Carsten Holbraad, "Both the declarations and the policies of Nikita Khrushchev and John Kennedy, the chief architects of detente ... suggest that neither the Soviet government nor the American administration considered a superpower condominium of the world a possible or even a desirable goal."[36] Admittedly, the prospect of a modern day Peace of Westphalia, as Ambassador Jacob Beam observes, is at odds with the fundamental ideological divide separating East and West.[37] However, a concert of sorts did develop between the United States and the Soviet Union in the period prior to and immediately after the consummation of the Limited Nuclear Test Ban Treaty. The dual threats of nuclear war and nuclear proliferation impelled Mr. Kennedy and Mr. Khrushchev to seek a truce in the Cold War and coexist competitively.

The Lessons Learned

There is no evidence that the members of EXCOM or other senior officials in the U.S. government gave much thought to the impact of the Cuban experience on the Soviets. Apprehension quickly gave way to an air of self-satisfaction. There seemed to be no doubt in Walt

Rostow's mind that Khrushchev's retreat was a product of the Kennedy Administration's foresight:

> When the nuclear threat failed to paralyze us, they [the Soviets] appear to have had neither the military concepts or plans to proceed on a military level.... On the other hand, we have been moving toward a doctrine of controlled conflict, even where a U.S.-U.S.S.R. confrontation of force is involved. What we have just passed through is, in fact, a first — and brilliantly improvised — exercise under that doctrine.[38]

Many in the administration would have agreed with Rostow's paean, but others offered their own explanations for the American victory.

In George Ball's view, the Soviets withdrew the missiles "because we had a clear superiority of conventional forces."[39] Mr. McNamara testified in 1963 that "Khrushchev knew without any question that he faced the full military power of the United States, including nuclear weapons.... We faced ... the possibility of launching nuclear weapons and Khrushchev knew it, and that is the reason, and the only reason, why he withdrew the weapons."[40] Two decades later, McNamara along with McGeorge Bundy and other former senior officials of the Kennedy Administration set forth the "The Lessons of the Cuban Missile Crisis" in an essay for *Time*. Among the ten lessons learned was the following:

> American nuclear superiority was not in our view a critical factor.... No one of us ever reviewed the nuclear balance for comfort in those hard weeks. The Cuban missile crisis illustrates not the significance but the insignificance of nuclear superiority in the face of survivable thermonuclear retaliatory forces. It also shows the crucial role of rapidly available conventional strength.[41]

Paul H. Nitze, a key insider during the 1962 crisis, had this to say about the issue:

> What was the cutting edge of our success in the missile crisis — was it that we dominated the seas around Cuba or was it our nuclear predominance? We dominated in both circumstances. The Russians and the Cubans didn't have a chance in the waters around Cuba. They couldn't escalate to a nuclear war because we had clear nuclear predominance.[42]

There is a fallacy in Mr. Nitze's logic. President Kennedy's nuclear threat of October 22, 1962, was directed against the launch of missiles from Cuba. It was not a threat to coerce the Soviets into removing them by placing the Soviet homeland at risk.[43]

McGeorge Bundy was much closer to the truth in 1964 than in 1983:

> Prudence argues for a judgment that all kinds of military strength were relevant. The existence of adequate and rapidly deployable strength, at all levels, was the direct result of the reinforcement of balanced defenses begun in 1961.[44]

This lesson was not lost on the Soviets. Khrushchev gave the Supreme Soviet a detailed and vivid account of the military preparations President Kennedy made in October 1962:

> Several airborne, infantry and armoured divisions, numbering about 100,000 men, were set aside just for an attack on Cuba. Moreover, 183 warships with 85,000 naval personnel were moved to the shores of Cuba. The landing on Cuba was to be covered by a few thousand military planes. Close to 20 per cent of all the planes of the U.S. Strategic Air Command were kept in the air round the clock, carrying atom and hydrogen bombs. Reservists were called up.[45]

The Cuban crisis had demonstrated to Khrushchev the dangers of relying solely on a missile deterrent to the detriment of conventional capabilities. He reluctantly announced on February 17, 1963, that the satisfaction of consumer needs would have to be deferred so that the regime could commit the "huge resources" needed to keep Soviet military power abreast of the Western powers.[46]

There is little question that the Cuban fiasco contributed to Khrushchev's political demise. The experience evidently persuaded his successors of the need to discard their predecessor's military strategy in favor of a balanced force posture. The Brezhnev-Kosygin-Podgorny triumvirate increased the pace of the expansion of Soviet military capabilities and gave meaning to an earlier warning to the United States by a senior Soviet diplomat, V.V. Kuznetsov: "We will not let you do this to us again."

Chapter 6
Conclusions

The great thing is to get the true picture whatever it is.
Winston Churchill

The crisis atmosphere that enveloped the superpowers during the early 1960s was a product of mistrust and misperception. The United States strove to contain the outward thrust of Soviet imperialism, and Stalin's successors were equally committed to breaking the capitalist encirclement of the Eastern bloc. Neither strategy required the opponent's cooperation. Nuclear deterrence simply reinforced two incompatible views of the strategic balance, or more precisely, the status quo.

The Kennedy Administration had neither the interest nor the inclination to fashion a political accommodation with the Soviets prior to the Cuban missile crisis. There was no appreciation of Khrushchev's fundamental conservatism in foreign affairs nor of his intense drive to secure for his nation the respect of the United States. The administration misread Khrushchev's attempts to bolster the legitimacy and stability of the Soviet bloc. Khrushchev's proposals on Berlin and Germany were taken as evidence of Soviet ambitions to fragment the North Atlantic Alliance and dominate Western Europe. The Munich legacy also hampered the administration's ability to recognize and exploit the diplomatic opportunities created by the Sino-Soviet conflict. President Kennedy's belief that the Soviets and the Chinese Communists presented a united front against American interests abroad found expression in his attempt to reinforce the truce lines of the Cold War. He equated the viability of nuclear deterrence with superior U.S. military capabilities.

Khrushchev's conception of nuclear deterrence was in line with his attempts to consolidate the Soviet hold on Eastern Europe and revitalize the Soviet economy. Khrushchev was satisfied with less than absolute nuclear parity with the United States as long as he could point

123

to some semblance of mutual deterrence. Like Stalin, he mortgaged Soviet foreign policy to the future growth of Soviet economic and military power. Unlike his patron, however, he was often too ready to parlay the perception of power to achieve his strategic objectives. Sputnik greatly enhanced Soviet prestige and emboldened Khrushchev to translate the success into tangible political gains at home and abroad. Khrushchev failed to realize, however, that by baiting the Eisenhower Administration with the specter of a "missile gap" in favor of the Soviets, he had also sowed the seeds for a vigorous American response. Khrushchev's deception only intensified American fears of a "nuclear" Pearl Harbor.

Sympathetic scholars and political admirers minimize President Kennedy's role in the "missile gap" controversy and argue that he was ignorant of the facts when he campaigned for office. Khrushchev certainly tried to foster the image of a "missile gap" in the aftermath of Sputnik with his own unique brand of boosterism and hyperbole. Khrushchev's rhetoric encouraged the U.S. intelligence community to pay more attention than was deserved to estimates of the number of missiles the Soviets could manufacture at full production. This preoccupation with capabilities overshadowed any critical examination of whether the Soviets actually intended to mount a massive expansion of their ICBM inventory. The U-2 program punctured the myth of the "bomber gap," but it failed to improve the learning curve of some members of the intelligence community as well as the Congress. Undaunted by its failure to demonstrate a serious Soviet long-range bomber threat, Air Force Intelligence quickly established its position on the high side of national estimates of the Soviet missile program. These grim prognostications fit smartly into the Strategic Air Command's efforts to win an even greater share of America's nuclear defense by increasing the size of its arsenal. Unfortunately, however, the Eisenhower Administration did not alert the American public to the relaxed pace of Soviet missile deployments until 1960. This belated acknowledgment was not enough to extricate the issue from the presidential campaign.

We still do not know with certainty when Kennedy realized that the "missile gap" was a fiction. Although not privy to U-2 imagery prior to his election, Kennedy was briefed on at least two occasions during the 1960 presidential campaign about Soviet missile developments. Ambition was clearly behind Kennedy's use of the "missile gap" to pummel the Eisenhower Administration for allegedly neglecting America's defenses. To fail to bolster U.S. military power threatened to leave the president open to the charge that he manufactured the entire issue. On the other hand, a prompt and public disavowal of the "missile gap" would have required more political courage than anyone in the administration, to include Mr. Kennedy, was willing to muster.

Nonetheless, Kennedy and his Secretary of Defense, Robert S. McNamara, moved ahead to strengthen the U.S. strategic nuclear deterrent for three reasons: first, to improve the survival of these forces; second, to garner immediate diplomatic advantages for the United States; and, third, to persuade the Soviets to accept an American definition of strategic stability based on the mutual vulnerability of their respective societies. The Soviets were clearly responsive to technical improvements in the quality of deterrence, and they were equally sensitive to the dangers of accidental war. However, Khrushchev and his military advisors adamantly refused to agree with McNamara's assertion that classical defenses were a dangerous anachronism in the nuclear age. Nor were the Soviets willing to subscribe to McNamara's various targeting improvisations such as the "No-Cities" doctrine. Ironically, the United States was no more secure after the Kennedy missile buildup than it was before.

There is still no satisfactory answer to the question of why Khrushchev sent ballistic missiles to Cuba. To this day, the Soviet Union has refused to alter its explanation that it was only acting to help Cuba to defend itself against American aggression. In this author's opinion, however, Khrushchev's plan was a bold gamble to restore some sense of equality to the strategic balance between the Soviet Union and the United States. The Kennedy Administration pressed its psychological advantage against Khrushchev in the wake of the Berlin crisis. Senior officials reminded the Soviets at every turn of the power and breadth of America's conventional and nuclear arsenal. The political objective of the campaign was to demonstrate that the U.S. could enforce the containment of the Soviet Union by military power alone. The rhetoric humiliated the Soviets. Khrushchev's retreat from the German peace treaty severely constrained his foreign policy options. Politically, he could not afford the opprobrium of strategic inferiority. Khrushchev had no guarantee that the U.S. would respect Soviet vital interests without some semblance of strategic deterrence. The Soviets responded with missiles in Cuba.

Each side came away from the Caribbean brink with a sober appreciation of the dangers of nuclear war and of their mutual stake in preventing this catastrophe. The experience set the stage for the limited detente that followed. The emergence of a more collaborative relationship between Washington and Moscow in the aftermath of the Cuban missile crisis was primarily a product of their mutual fear of nuclear proliferation in general, and of Communist China in particular. As de Gaulle's France and Mao's China pulled away from their respective political orbits, the United States and the Soviet Union were drawn closer together by a common concern with protecting their duopolistic dominance of world affairs. The final negotiations leading to a Limited Nuclear Test Ban Treaty became the vehicle for their collaboration.

The political interactions between Kennedy and Khrushchev were complemented by the policies of their ministers of defense. Robert McNamara and Rodion Malinovskiy typified the mainstream of strategic thought in their respective countries; McNamara, the technocratic manager preoccupied with the problem of force levels and cost effectiveness, and Malinovskiy, the hardened combat veteran concerned just as much with the realities of the battlefield. The obvious differences between the men frequently obscure the fact that they shared a series of common concerns if not perspectives. Both men faced the problem of asserting their leadership in a competitive bureaucratic environment and fashioning a unified defense policy. McNamara enforced unity by the strength of his own personality, the complete support of the president, and his absolute control of the preparation of the defense budget. The published record still provides only brief glimpses of the bureaucratic strife Malinovskiy faced. Nor do we know how Malinovskiy managed to create a consensus of opinion between proponents of Khrushchev's fledgling Strategic Rocket Forces, and the tradition-bound generals of the Soviet Ground Froces. The eventual agreement had something for everyone. Missiles were deemed to be decisive in a short, intense war, and a sizable conventional force were declared to be essential in a protracted conflict. Malinovskiy wisely took care that the debate never included direct criticisms of Khrushchev's political acumen or the prerogatives of the Communist Party.

McNamara and Malinovskiy shared a second important concern: what to do if nuclear deterrence failed. Malinovskiy had no better idea of how to wage and win a nuclear war than his American counterpart. McNamara tried to finesse the risks and uncertainties by propounding the dictum of assured destruction, which was not a strategy, but a formula for national suicide. Terror attacks against the enemy's civilian centers were no less important to the Soviet conception of nuclear deterrence. The difference, however, was that Khrushchev and his marshals insisted on providing some protection for the Soviet population no matter how marginal the prospects for survival in a nuclear conflict.

Past comparisons of U.S. and Soviet defense policy have typically run aground on the definitional differences between deterrence and defense. Proponents of deterrence see no value in nuclear weapons other than to prevent a first strike by either superpower. The supporters of defense, on the other hand, champion a strategy of victory in nuclear war and assert the value of nuclear weapons as instruments of coercive diplomacy.

This distinction may be analytically elegant, but it offers little insight into the essence of the strategic competition between the United States and the Soviet Union. Nuclear deterrence has never been a matter of choice for either superpower, but rather a condition of their relationship. What then can be said about the nature of nuclear deterrence during the Kennedy and Khrushchev years? In the first place, both men tried to secure immediate political benefits from nuclear weapons and failed. The reason is simple. Neither believed that the other would sanction their use for anything less than the ultimate defense of their homelands. However, the strategic balance remained unstable as long as both sides refused to acknowledge their equality as superpowers and their common stake in the avoidance of nuclear war.

Notes

Introduction

1. U.S. Congress, House Committee on Appropriations, *Department of Defense Appropriations for FY 1964: Hearings before the Subcommittee on Defense Appropriations, Part I*, 88th Cong., 1st sess., 1963, p. 513.

2. Roman Kolkowicz, "Strategic Parity and Beyond—Soviet Perspectives," *World Politics* 23 (April 1971): 439–440.

3. Johan J. Holst, *Comparative U.S. and Soviet Deployments, Doctrines and Arms Limitations* (Chicago: University of Chicago Press, 1971), p. 5.

4. Benjamin S. Lambeth, *The Elements of Soviet Strategic Policy* (Santa Monica, CA: Rand Corporation, 1979), p. 8.

5. James L. Buckley and Paul C. Warnke, *Strategic Sufficiency: Fact or Fiction* (Washington, D.C.: American Enterprise Institute, 1972), pp. 3 and 12.

6. *Ibid.*, pp. 23 and 37.

7. Paul H. Nitze, "Deterring Our Deterrent," *Foreign Policy* 25 (Winter 1976–77): 206–207.

8. Colin S. Gray and Keith Payne, "Victory Is Possible," *Foreign Policy* 39 (Summer 1980): 20–21.

9. "The Real Paul Warnke," *The New Republic* (March 26, 1977): 23.

10. Richard Pipes, "Why the Soviet Union Thinks It Could Fight and Win a Nuclear War," *Commentary* 64 (July 1977): 21–22.

11. John Erickson, "The Chimera of Mutual Deterrence," *Strategic Review* (Spring 1978): 11–12 and 14.

12. Raymond L. Garthoff, "Mutual Deterrence and Strategic Arms Limitation in Soviet Policy," *International Security* 3 (Winter 1980–81): 146 and 112–113.

The Pipes-Garthoff debate received its fullest exposition four years later on the pages of *Strategic Review* (Fall 1982). Mutual recrimination aside, the basic difference between them turns on the answer to a simple, but vital question: Is the Soviet Union an expansionist power?

13. Bernard Brodie, "The Development of Nuclear Strategy," *International Security* 2 (Spring 1978): 78 and 79.

14. Michael E. Howard, "On Fighting a Nuclear War," *International Security* 5 (Spring 1981): 14.

15. Robert Legvold, "Strategic 'Doctrine' and SALT: Soviet and American Views," *Survival* 21 (January–February 1979): 8.

16. Fritz W. Ermarth, "Contrasts in American and Soviet Strategic Thought," *International Security* 3 (Fall 1978): 139.

17. Ken Booth, *Strategy and Enthnocentrism* (New York: Holmes and Meier, 1979), pp. 142 and 147.

Chapter 1. Kennedy, Khrushchev and the Cold War

1. James MacGregor Burns, *John F. Kennedy: A Political Profile* (New York: Harcourt, Brace, 1959), p. 38.

2. Charles E. Bohlen, *Witness to History 1929–1969* (New York: W.W. Norton, 1973), p. 476.

3. John F. Kennedy, *Why England Slept*, 2nd ed. (New York: Wilfred Funk, 1961), pp. 230–231.

4. Herbert S. Parmet, *J.F.K.: The Presidency of John F. Kennedy*, (New York: Dial, 1983), p. 73.

5. Herbert Goldhamer, *Political Implications of Posture Choices*, RM-2683 (Santa Monica, CA: Rand Corporation, 1960), pp. 7–8 and p. 13. (Emphasis in the original.) John F. Kennedy Library, Presidential Office Files, Box 64. (Hereafter referred to as JFKL, POF.)

6. Dean Rusk, interview held in Athens, Georgia, March 2, 1984.

7. Raymond Garthoff, "Military Power in Soviet Policy," in *The Military-Technical Revolution: Its Impact on Strategy and Foreign Policy*, ed. John Erickson (New York: Frederick A. Praeger, 1966), p. 243.

8. Isaac Deutscher, *Russia, China, and the West: A Contemporary Chronical 1953–1966* (London: Oxford University Press, 1970), p. 69.

9. Leo Gruliow, ed., *Current Soviet Policies I: The Documentary Record of the 20th Communist Party and Its Aftermath* (New

York: Frederick A. Praeger, 1957), p. 35.

10. Central Intelligence Agency Report, *Khrushchev—A Personality Sketch*, OCI No. 2391/61, pp. 1-2. JFKL, POF, Box 126.

11. *Ibid.*, p. 8.

12. Strobe Talbott, ed., *Khrushchev Remembers* (Boston: Little, Brown, 1970), p. 395.

13. John F. Kennedy, *The Strategy of Peace* (New York: Harper and Brothers, 1960), p. 9.

14. Deutscher, pp. 181-182.

15. "Poslaniye Predsedatelya Soveta Ministrov SSSR N.S. Khrushcheva—Kantseru FRG Adenaueru," *Pravda*, February 2, 1960, p. 2.

16. "Deklaratsiya gosudarstv—uchactnikov Varshavskovo dogovora," *Pravda*, February 5, 1960, p. 2.

17. "Priyem N.S. Khrushchevym delegatsiy bratskikh partiy sotsialisticheskikh stran," *Pravda*, February 6, 1960, p. 1.

18. "Val'ter Ul'brikht: Za mirnoe reshenie germanskoy problemy," *Sovetskaya Rossiya*, February 7, 1960, p. 3.

19. Foreign Broadcast Information Service, U.S.S.R. Daily Report, May 19, 1960, p. BB-6.

20. Foreign Broadcast Information Service, U.S.S.R. Daily Report, June 22, 1960, p. JJ-26.

21. Bohlen, p. 475.

22. U.S. Congress, Senate Committee on Commerce, *The Speeches, Remarks, Press Conferences, and Statements of Senator John F. Kennedy, August 1 through November 7, 1960, S. Report. 994, Part I*, 87th Cong., 1st sess., 1961, pp. 1157-1158.

23. U.S. Congress, Senate Committee on Commerce, *The Joint Appearances of Senator John F. Kennedy and Vice President Richard M. Nixon and Other 1960 Campaign Presentations, S. Rept. 994, Part III*, 87th Cong., 1st sess., 1961, p. 159.

24. Roy E. Medvedev, *Khrushchev* (New York: Anchor/Doubleday, 1983), p. 154.

25. *Keesing's Contemporary Archives* (London: 1960-1961), p. 17931.

26. Foreign Broadcast Information Service, U.S.S.R. Daily Report, October 21, 1960, p. BB-15.

27. "Telegramma Gospodinu Dzhonu F. Kennedi," *Pravda*, November 10, 1960, p. 1.

28. Letter, W. Averell Harriman to John F. Kennedy, November 12, 1960, JFKL, POF, Box 125.

29. Letter, W. Averell Harriman to John F. Kennedy, November

15, 1960, JFKL, POF, Box 125.

30. Letter, Adlai Stevenson to John F. Kennedy, November 22, 1960, JFKL, POF, Box 125.

31. Memorandum of Conversation, W. Averell Harriman with Mikhail Menshikov, November 21, 1960, JFKL, POF, Box 125.

32. Memorandum of Conversation, W. Averell Harriman with Mikhail Menshikov, December 14, 1960, JFKL, POF, Box 125.

33. *Facts on File*, 21 (January 5–11, 1961): 2.

The two RB-47 fliers were released shortly after the inauguration. Khrushchev subsequently told Drew Pearson that he had refused to free the men during the presidential election campaign because he thought the gesture might have helped to elect Mr. Nixon.

34. *Facts on File*, 21 (January 19–25, 1961): 24.

35. D.C. Watt, *Survey of International Affairs 1961* (London: Oxford University Press, 1965), p. 213.

36. N.S. Khrushchev, *Communism — Peace and Happiness for the People, I*, January — September 1961 (Moscow: Foreign Language Publishing House, 1963), pp. 19 and 43.

37. State Department Airgram, January 24, 1961, JFKL, POF, Box 125A.

38. State Department Telegram, January 19, 1961, pp. 1–2, JFKL, National Security Files, Box 176. (Hereafter referred to as NSF.)

39. State Department Telegram, Part II, February 2, 1961, pp. 1–4, JFKL, NSF, Box 176.

40. Murray Marder, "Kennedy Is Not Encouraging Khrushchev Visit to the U.N.," *Washington Post*, January 29, 1961, p. A-6.

41. State Department Telegram, Part I, February 2, 1961, pp. 2–3, JFKL, NSF, Box 176.

42. David Halberstam, *The Best and the Brightest* (New York: Random House, 1972), p. 122.

43. Stewart Alsop, "Kennedy's Grand Strategy," *Saturday Evening Post*, 235 (March 31, 1962): 12.

44. U.S. President, *Public Papers of the President of the United States* (Washington, D.C.: Government Printing Office, 1962), John F. Kennedy, January 20 to December 31, 1961, p. 23.

To add punch to his rhetoric, President Kennedy asked his National Security Council to prepare a report on the possibilities of establishing a $1 billion Freedom Fund to be administered under the direct supervision of the president to support various Cold War operations. The president subsequently accepted his Budget Bureau's recommendation to request an increase in military aid appropriations and greater presidential discretionary authority instead. See Draft Record of Actions, 478th N.S.C. Mtg, April 22, 1961, and Bureau of the Budget, Freedom Fund Evaluation, Lyndon Baines Johnson Library, Vice Presidential Security Files, Box 4. (Hereafter referred to as LBJL, VPSF.)

45. *Facts on File*, 21 (February 16–22, 1961): 61.

46. Memorandum, Walter Stoessel, Jr., to Brigadier General Clifton, February 17, 1961, JFKL, NSF, Box 176.

47. Memorandum, W. Walt Rostow to John F. Kennedy, February 16, 1961, JFKL, NSF, Box 176.

48. Watt, p. 218.

49. Letter and Enclosure, Harry Schwartz to W. Walt Rostow, March 4, 1961, JFKL, NSF, Box 176.

50. "Soviet Challenge—and U.S. Moves to Counter It," *New York Times*, April 2, 1961, p. E-2.

51. Watt, p. 216.

52. Walter Lippmann, *The Coming Tests with Russia* (Boston: Little, Brown, 1961), p. 27.

53. Letter, N.S. Khrushchev to John F. Kennedy, April 18, 1961, JFKL, NSF, Box 180.

54. *Public Papers on the President of the United States—1961*, p. 306.

55. *Ibid.*, p. 336.

56. State Department Telegram, May 4, 1961, JFKL, NSF, Box 176.

57. Kenneth P. O'Donnell and David F. Powers, *Johnny, We Hardly Knew Ye* (Boston: Little, Brown, 1970), p. 286.

58. State Department Memorandum of Conversation, May 16, 1961, JFKL, NSF, Box 176.

59. Arthur M. Schlesinger, Jr., *A Thousand Days* (New York: Fawcett Premier, 1965), p. 326.

60. State Department Special Background Paper, "Line of Approach to Khrushchev," June 1, 1961, pp. 1–2, *The Declassified Documents Quarterly Catalog* 2 (Oct–Dec 1976): 293.

61. Bohlen, p. 481.

62. Schlesinger, pp. 334–336.

63. Hugh Sidey, *John F. Kennedy, President* (New York: Atheneum, 1964), p. 200.

64. O'Donnell and Powers, p. 298.

65. Halberstam, p. 76.

66. O'Donnell and Powers, p. 299.

67. Quoted by Helen Fuller, *Year of Trial: Kennedy's Crucial*

Decisions (New York: Harcourt, Brace & World, 1962), pp. 235–236.

68. Foreign Broadcast Information Service, U.S.S.R. Daily Report, June 22, 1961, p. BB-6.

69. Foreign Broadcast Information Service, U.S.S.R. Daily Report, July 10, 1961, p. BB-21.

70. Alexander L. George and Richard L. Smoke, *Deterrence and American Foreign Policy* (New York: Columbia University Press, 1974, pp. 433–434.

71. *Public Papers of the President of the United States — 1961*, pp. 534–537.

72. James E. McSherry, *Khrushchev and Kennedy in Retrospect* (Palo Alto, CA: Open Door Press, 1971), p. 74.

73. State Department Telegram, August 8, 1961, JFKL, POF, Box 125A.

74. President's Intelligence Checklist, August 21, 1961, *The Declassified Documents Quarterly Catalog* 1 (April–June 1975): 52.

75. Foreign Broadcast Information Service, U.S.S.R. Daily Report, August 7, 1961, p. BB-8.

76. Foreign Broadcast Information Service, U.S.S.R. Daily Report, August 14, 1961, pp. 33–35.

77. In his memoirs, Khrushchev claims that Konev's appointment was only "administrative" in order to demonstrate to the Americans Soviet seriousness in Berlin. Konev, he writes, spent most of his time in Moscow. Talbott, p. 459.

78. Oral History Interview with Lyman Lemnitzer, February 11, 1970 by David Nunnerly, John F. Kennedy Library, p. 4.

79. Oral History Interview with W. Walt Rostow, April 11, 1964 (Second Session) by Richard Neustadt, John F. Kennedy Library, pp. 60–61.

80. U.S. President, *Public Papers of the President of the United States* (Washington, D.C.: Government Printing Office, 1963), John F. Kennedy, January 20 to December 31, 1962, pp. 20–21.

81. Talbott, p. 454.

82. Seymour Topping, "Khrushchev Says Prestige Compels a German Treaty," *New York Times*, August 12, 1961, p. 3.

83. Charlotte Saikowski and Leo Gruliow, eds., *Current Soviet Policies IV: The Documentary Record of the 22nd Congress of the Communist Party of the Soviet Union* (New York: Fredrick A. Praeger, 1952), p. 174.

84. N. Inozemtsev, "Mirnoe Sosushchestvovanie — Vazhneyshiy Vopros Sovremennosti," *Pravda*, January 17, 1962, p. 5.

85. Paul H. Nitze, "The World Situation," September 7, 1961, in

Vital Speeches 28 (October 15, 1961): 26-27.

86. James Reston, "President Is Undertaking Review of Foreign Policy," *New York Times*, September 25, 1961, p. 4.

87. Nitze, p. 27.

88. Foreign Broadcast Information Service, U.S.S.R. Daily Report, May 31, 1960, p. BB-30.

Chapter 2. The Strategists: McNamara and Malinovskiy

1. *The Speeches, Remarks, Press Conferences and Statements of Senator John F. Kennedy, August 1 Through November 7, 1960*, p. 980.

2. *Public Papers of the President of the United States—1961*, pp. 23-24.

3. Ernest J. Yanarella, *The Missile Defense Controversy* (Lexington: The University Press of Kentucky, 1977), pp. 42-43.

4. O'Donnell and Powers, p. 327.

5. Oral History Interview with Colonel Thomas W. Wolfe, October 30, 1970 by William M. Ross, John F. Kennedy Library, p. 19.

6. Walter D. Jacobs, "Marshal Malinovskiy and Missiles," *Military Review* 50 (June 1960): 20.

7. Thomas W. Wolfe, *Soviet Strategy at the Crossroads* (Cambridge: Harvard University Press, 1965), p. 33.

8. Quoted by Michael Howard, "Classical Strategists," in *Problems of Modern Strategy* (New York: Frederick A. Praeger, 1970), p. 61.

9. Herbert S. Dinerstein, *War and the Soviet Union* (Santa Monica, CA: Rand Corporation), pp. 6-7.

10. John Foster Dulles, "The Evolution of Foreign Policy," *The Bulletin of the Department of State* 30 (January 25, 1954): 108.

11. John Foster Dulles, "Policy for Security and Peace," *Foreign Affairs* 32 (April 1954): 338 and 363.

12. Howard, p. 62.

13. Albert Wohlstetter, "The Delicate Balance of Terror," *Foreign Affairs* 37 (January 1959): 230.

14. Bernard Brodie, "Implications for Military Policy," in *The Absolute Weapon*, ed. Bernard Brodie (New York: Harcourt, Brace, 1946), p. 76.

15. *Ibid*.

16. Bernard Brodie, *Strategy in the Missile Age* (New Jersey: Princeton University Press, 1959), p. 293.

17. *Ibid.*, p. 396.

18. Herman Kahn, *On Thermonuclear War* (New Jersey: Princeton University Press, 1960), p. 96. (Emphasis in original.)

19. *Ibid.*, p. 90.

20. *Ibid.*, pp. 174–175.

21. *Public Papers of the President of the United States—1961*, pp. 231–232.

22. Thomas Powers, "Choosing a Strategy for World War III," *The Atlantic* 250 (November 1982): 92.

23. *Ibid.*, p. 93.

24. Paul Bracken, *The Command and Control of Nuclear Forces* (New Haven, CT: Yale University Press, 1983), p. 85.

25. U.S. Congress, House Committee on Appropriations, *Department of Defense Appropriations for FY 1963: Hearings Before the Subcommittee on Defense Appropriations, Part II*, 87th Cong., 2nd sess., 1962, pp. 249–250.

26. Quoted by William L. Kaufmann, *The McNamara Strategy* (New York: Harper and Row, 1964), p. 73.

27. *Ibid.*, p. 114.

28. Memorandum, Robert S. McNamara to Dean Rusk, May 31, 1962, JFKL, POF, Box 117.

29. Memorandum, McGeorge Bundy to John F. Kennedy, June 1, 1962, JFKL, POF, Box 117.

30. Reprinted by the *New York Times*, June 17, 1962, p. 26.

31. May 30, 1962, Draft Remarks for University of Michigan Commencement, p. 11, JFKL, POF, Box 117.

32. Marquis Childs, "McNamara Denies First-Strike Aim," *Washington Post*, July 13, 1962, p. A-18.

33. Michael Brower, "Controlled Thermonuclear War," *New Republic* (July 30, 1962): 13.

34. Morton H. Halperin, "The 'No Cities' Doctrine," *New Republic* (October 8, 1962): 18–19.

35. Marshal V.D. Sokolovskiy, "Strategiya Samoubiyts," *Krasnaya Zvezda*, July 19, 1962, p. 4.

36. *Department of Defense Appropriations for FY 1964*, p. 109.

37. *Ibid.*, p. 111.

38. U.S. Congress, House Committee on Appropriations, *Department of Defense Appropriations for FY 1965: Hearings Before the Subcommittee on Defense Appropriations*, 88th Cong., 2nd sess., 1964, p. 27.

39. Dinerstein, pp. 39 and 47.

40. *Ibid.*, p. 51.

41. Colonel I. Korotkov, "O razvitii sovetskoy voennoy teorii v poslevoennyye gody," *Voenno-Istoricheskiy Zhurnal* (April, 1964): pp. 40 and 42.

42. *Ibid.*, p. 44.

43. *Ibid.*

44. *Ibid.*, pp. 46–47. (Emphasis in original.)

45. *Ibid.*, p. 47.

46. Wolfe, pp. 6–7.

47. Gruliow, *Current Soviet Policies I*, p. 37.

48. Talbott, p. 408.

49. Quoted by Michael P. Gehlen, *The Politics of Coexistence* (Bloomington: Indiana University Press, 1967), p. 72.

50. Preston Grover, "Khrushchev Twits General at Party," *Washington Post*, November 9, 1959, p. A-1.

51. A.I. Goldberg, "Reds Hint Unilateral Cut in Army," *Washington Post*, January 2, 1960, p. A-1.

52. Total Soviet troop strength was reduced, between 1955 and 1960, from 5,763,000 to 3,623,000. Khrushchev later claimed that this reduction was made possible by the establishment of the Warsaw Pact. See Strobe Talbott, *Khrushchev Remembers: The Last Testament* (Boston: Little, Brown, 1974), p. 220. The burden of these cuts fell primarily on the ground forces. However, these economies did not reduce the number of Soviet divisions. See also J.M. Mackintosh, *Strategy and Tactics of Soviet Foreign Policy* (London: Oxford University Press, 1962), p. 104.

53. Marshal V.D. Sokolovskiy, *Soviet Military Strategy*, translation and analytic introduction by Herbert S. Dinerstein, Leon Goure and Thomas W. Wolfe (Englewood Cliffs, NJ: Prentice-Hall, Inc., 1963), p. 14. (Unless noted otherwise, all references to *Military Strategy* refer to this Rand Corporation translation.)

54. V.F. Tolubko, *Nedelin* (Moscow: Molodaya Gvardiya, 1979), p. 188.

55. N.I. Savinkin and K.M. Bogolyubov, *KPSS o Vooruzhennykh Silakh Sovetskovo Soyuza* (Moscow: Voenizdat, 1981), p. 369.

56. N.S. Khrushchev, "Disarmament—The Way to a Sure Peace and Friendly Relations Between Peoples," *Pravda*, 15 January 1960, translated by *The Current Digest of the Soviet Press* 12 (February 10, 1960): 13.

57. *Ibid.*, p. 10.

58. *Ibid.*, p. 11.

59. *Ibid.*

According to George Breslauer, Khrushchev apparently was not concerned with a redistribution of economic resources when he made his 1960 decision to reduce troop strength. His intention was rather to hold down manpower expenditures within the military budget so as to finance increases in other components of the military budget, namely, strategic and tactical weapons development. See George W. Breslauer, *Khrushchev and Brezhnev* (London: George Allen and Unwin, 1982), p. 69.

60. *Ibid.*, p. 14.

61. Marshal R. Ya. Malinovskiy, "Na Strazhe Mira," *Pravda*, February 23, 1960, p. 2.

62. Harriet F. Scott and William F. Scott, *The Armed Forces of the U.S.S.R.* (Boulder, CO: Westview, 1970), p. 43.

63. Walter C. Clemens, Jr., "The Soviet Militia in the Missile Age," *Orbis* 8 (Spring 1964): 92.

64. Walter C. Clemens, Jr., "Soviet Disarmament Proposals and the Cadre-Territorial Army," *Orbis* 7 (Winter 1963): 799.

65. Sokolovskiy was relieved by General M.V. Zakharov in April 1960 as Chief of the General Staff and Konev was replaced the same month by General A.A. Grechko as Commander of the Warsaw Pact Forces. However, there was no diminution of their political ranking during the remainder of Khrushchev's rule. Sokolovskiy remained a candidate member of the Central Committee and Konev continued as a full member of that body.

66. U.S. Congress, Senate Committee on Foreign Relations, *Hearings on Strategic Arms Limitation*, 92nd Cong., 2nd sess., 1972, p. 333.

67. Harry Schwartz, "The Spy Who Came in from the Cold," *Saturday Review* 49 (January 29, 1966): 36.

68. Walter Laqueur, "Spies," *New York Review of Books* 5 (January 30, 1966): 6.

69. Thomas W. Wolfe, "Review," *Journal of Modern History* 38 (June 1966): 237.

70. Oleg P. Penkovskiy, *The Penkovskiy Papers* (New York: Doubleday, 1965), p. 257.

71. *Ibid.*, p. 258.

72. *Ibid.*, p. 227.

73. *Ibid.*, pp. 254–255. (Emphasis in original.)

74. "Rech' deputata R. Ya. Malinovskovo," *Izvestia*, January 16, 1960, p. 2.

75. *Ibid.*

76. Major General N.A. Talenskiy, "The Character of Modern Wars," *International Affairs* (October 1960): 24.

77. Colonel A.M. Iovlev, "Novaya tekhnika i massovyye armii," *Krasnaya Zvezda*, April 5, 1961, p. 2.

78. Foreign Broadcast Information Service, U.S.S.R. Daily Report, October 4, 1961, p. BB-20.

79. Foreign Broadcast Information Service, U.S.S.R. Daily Report, November 15, 1961, p. BB-29.

80. Quoted by Nikolai Galay, "The Soviet Approach to the Modern Military Revolution," in *The Military—Technical Revolution*, ed. by John Erickson (New York: Frederick A. Praeger, 1966), pp. 22–23.

81. Sokolovskiy, p. 82.

82. *Ibid.*, p. 93.

83. *Ibid.*, p. 95.

84. *Ibid.*, p. 302.

85. *Ibid.*, p. 314. (Emphasis in original.)

86. *Ibid.*, p. 339.

87. *Ibid.*, p. 95.

88. Marshal V.D. Sokolovskiy, *Voennaya Strategiya* with an analytic introduction by Raymond L. Garthoff (London: Pall Mall, 1963), p. xx.

89. Admiral V.A. Alafuzov "K vykhodu v svet truda *Voennaya Strategia,*" *Morskoy Sbornik* (January 1963): 88 and 94.

90. General P.A. Kurochkin, *Voennaya Strategia, Krasnaya Zvezda*, September 22, 1962, p. 2.

91. A. Golubev, "O nekotorykh voprosakh voennoy istorii v knige *Voennaya Strategia,*" *Voenno-Istoricheskiy Zhurnal* (May 1963): 101.

92. Colonel V. Zemskov and Colonel A. Yakimovskiy, *Voennaya Strategia, Voenyy Vestnik* (January 1963): 124.

93. Sokolvskiy, pp. 130–131.

94. Marshal R. Ya. Malinovskiy, *Bditel'no Stoyat Ha Strazhe Mira* (Moscow: Voenizdat, 1963), pp. 16 and 22.

95. Colonel A. Belousov, "Konferentsiya O Sovetskoy Voennoy Doktrina," *Voenno-Istoricheskiy Zhurnal* (October, 1963): 121–126.

96. Colonel General N.A. Lomov, *Voennaya Sovetskaya Doktrina* (Moscow: Voenizdat, 1963), trans. by the Joint Publications Research Service, No. 21678, October 31, 1963, p. 4.

97. Marshal V.D. Sokolovskiy, *Soviet Military Strategy*, 3rd ed., trans. by Harriet F. Scott (New York: Crane, Rusak, 1975), p. xlii.

98. Robert D. Crane, *Soviet Nuclear Strategy* (Washington DC: Georgetown Center for Strategic Studies, 1963), p. 1.

99. *Ibid.*, pp. 7 and 10.

100. *Department of Defense Appropriations for FY 1964*, pp. 513–514.

101. Memorandum for the Record, Presentation by General Thomas S. Powers, April 28, 1964, LBJL, NSF, Box 12.

102. Hanson W. Baldwin, "Stalemate — On?" *U.S. Naval Institute* Proceedings 9 (April 1964): 55.

103. Talbott, *Khrushchev Remembers*, p. 518.

Chapter 3. The Preconditions for Deterrence

1. Central Intelligence Agency, *Compendium of Soviet Remarks on Missiles*, p. 2g, JFKL, NSF, Box 176.

2. Quoted by Mark E. Miller, *Soviet Strategic Power and Doctrine: The Quest for Superiority* (Washington, D.C.: Advanced International Studies Institute, 1982), p. 25.

3. Talbott, *Khrushchev Remembers: The Last Testament*, p. 26.

4. *Ibid.*, p. 43.

5. *Compendium of Soviet Remarks on Missiles*, p. 2h.

6. *Ibid.*, p. 2i.

7. Allen W. Dulles, *The Craft of Intelligence* (New York: Harper and Row, 1963), p. 163.

8. Dulles, p. 149.

9. Arnold L. Horelick and Myron Rush, *Strategic Power and Soviet Foreign Policy* (Santa Monica, CA: Rand Corporation, 1965), p. 57.

10. *Compendium of Soviet Remarks on Missiles*, p. 2n.

11. Foreign Service Dispatch, June 26, 1959, p. 7, JFKL, POF, Box 126.

12. Richard M. Nixon, *Leaders* (N.Y.: Warner, 1982), p. 190.

13. N.S. Khrushchev, "Disarmament — The Way to a Secure Peace and Friendly Relations Between Peoples," p. 10.

14. Holst, p. 33.

15. Lieutenant General James M. Gavin, *War and Peace in the Space Age* (New York: Harper and Brothers, 1958), p. 4.

16. Joseph Alsop, "A Very Big Issue," *Washington Post*, August 18, 1959, p. A-11.

17. Herbert S. Parmet, *Jack: The Struggles of John F. Kennedy* (New York: Dial, 1980), pp. 446–447.

18. Kennedy, *The Strategy of Peace*, p. 43.

19. *Ibid.*, pp. 37–38.

20. Henry L. Trewitt, *McNamara: His Ordeal in the Pentagon* (New York: Harper and Row, 1971), p. 6.

Theodore Sorenson contends that Kennedy was never presented with the U-2 evidence in the CIA and military briefings he received during the campaign and he also claims that Kennedy handled the "missile gap" issue judiciously. See Theodore C. Sorenson, *Kennedy* (New York: Harper and Row, 1965), p. 612.

21. Oral History Interview with Earle Wheeler, 1964, by Chester Clifton, John F. Kennedy Library, p. 2.

22. *The Speeches, Remarks, Press Conferences, and Statements of Senator John F. Kennedy, August 1 Through November 7, 1960*, p. 1165.

23. Trewitt, p. 6.

24. *The Speeches, Remarks, Press Conferences and Statements of Senator John F. Kennedy, August 1, Through November 7, 1960*, p. 1165.

25. Desmond Ball, *Politics and Force Levels: The Strategic Missile Program of the Kennedy Administration* (Berkeley: University of California Press, 1950), p. 55.

26. Holst, p. 7.

27. Thomas W. Wolfe, *The Global Strategic Perspective from Moscow* (Santa Monica, CA: Rand Corporation, 1973), p. 7.

28. U.S. Department of Defense, *Annual Report for 1961* (Washington, D.C.: Government Printing Office, 1962), pp. 7–8.

29. Robert S. McNamara, *The Essence of Security: Reflections in Office* (New York: Harper & Row, 1968), pp. 57–58.

30. *Ibid.*, pp. 58 and 60.

31. James Bamford, *The Puzzle Palace: A Report on America's Most Secret Agency* (Boston: Houghton Mifflin, 1982), p. 187.

32. Schlesinger, p. 324.

33. State Department Telegram, January 30, 1961, pp. 1–2, JFKL, POF, Box 125A.

34. Bamford, p. 188.

35. Ball, p. 101.

36. *Public Papers of the President of the United States — 1961*, p. 67.

37. *Facts on File* (February 9–15, 1961), p. 54.

38. Letter, Allen W. Dulles to McGeorge Bundy, February 28, 1961, JFKL, NSF, Box 176.

39. *Public Papers of the President of the United States — 1961*, p. 231.

40. *Ibid.*, pp. 231–232.

41. *Ibid.*, pp. 233–235.

42. U.S. Congress, House Committee on Appropriations,

Department of Defense Appropriations for 1962: Hearings Before the Subcommittee on Defense Appropriations, Part III, 87th Cong., 1st sess., 1961, pp. 59–60.

43. *Ibid.*, p. 112.

44. Ball, p. xxvi.

45. *Ibid.*, pp. 177, 178 and 211.

46. Philip J. Klass, *Secret Sentries in Space* (New York: Random House, 1971), p. 109.

47. Summary Minutes of the 501st National Security Council Meeting, July 9, 1962, pp. 1–2, JFKL, NSF, Box 313.

48. Memorandum, John F. Kennedy to McGeorge Bundy, February 11, 1963, JFKL, NSF, Box 298.

49. Memorandum, Robert S. McNamara to John F. Kennedy, March 4, 1963, pp. 1 and 5, JFKL, NSF, Box 298.

50. Bundy Handwritten Note, March 4, 1963, JFKL, NSF, Box 298. (Emphasis in original.)

51. Memorandum, Adam Yarmolinskiy to McGeorge Bundy, March 15, 1963, JFKL, NSF, Box 298. (Emphasis in original.)

52. Memorandum, Tazewell Shepard to McGeorge Bundy, March 30, 1963, JFKL, NSF, Box 298.

53. Letter, Paul H. Nitze to McGeorge Bundy, May 30, 1963, JFKL, NSF, Box 298, and Memorandum, Lawrence C. McQuade to Paul H. Nitze, May 31, 1963, pp. 21–22, JFKL, NSF, Box 298.

54. Letter, Paul H. Nitze to McGeorge Bundy, June 17, 1963, p. 2, JFKL, NSF, Box 298.

55. McNamara, p. 59.

56. *Department of Defense Appropriations for 1962*, p. 18.

57. *Ibid.*, p. 134.

58. Ball, p. 102.

59. McQuade Memorandum, pp. 14–15.

60. Andrew Tully, *The Super Spies* (New York: William Morrow, 1969), p. 35.

61. John A. Loftus, "Gilpatric Warns US Can Destroy Atom Aggressor," *New York Times*, October 22, 1961, pp. 1 and 6.

62. Max Frankel, "Rusk Says Stronger U.S. Is Ready to Meet Russians," *New York Times*, October 21, 1962, pp. 1 and 3.

63. Quoted by George E. Lowe, *The Age of Deterrence* (Boston: Little, Brown, 1964), p. 240.

64. *Department of Defense Appropriations for 1963*, pp. 20 & 27.

65. Trewitt, p. 115.

66. Oral History Interview with Roswell Gilpatric, May 1970, by Dennis J. O'Brien, John F. Kennedy Library, p. 118.

67. Quoted by Ball, p. 179.

68. Hansen W. Baldwin, "Russian Missiles Guarded by Concrete Installations," *New York Times*, July 26, 1962, pp. 1 and 2.

69. Edward Klein and Robert Littel, "Sh! Let's Tell the Russians," *Newsweek* (May 5, 1969): 46.

70. Gilpatric Oral History Interview, p. 77.

71. Dean Rusk, interview held in Athens, Georgia, March 2, 1984.

72. John T. McNaughton, "Arms Restraint in Military Decisions," *The Journal of Conflict Resolution* 7 (1963): 228.

73. *Ibid.*, p. 328.

74. Gilpatric Oral History Interview, p. 77.

75. Holst, p. 24.

76. M.A. Mil'shteyn and A.K. Slobodenko, *Concerning the Military Doctrine of the USA* (Moscow: Znanie, 1963), trans. by Kenneth R. Whiting, *Soviet Reactions to American Military Strategy* (Montgomery: Air University, 1965), p. 88.

77. Stewart Alsop, "Our New Strategy: The Alternative to Total War," *Saturday Evening Post* 236 (December 1, 1962): 14.

78. Wolfe, *Soviet Strategy at the Crossroads*, p. 41.

79. I. Glagolev and V. Larionov, "Soviet Defense Might and Peaceful Coexistence," *International Affairs* (November 1963): 31–32.

80. Federal Emergency Management Agency, *American Civil Defense 1945–1975* (Washington, D.C., 1980), p. 309.

81. *Ibid.*, pp. 385–386.

82. Benson D. Adams, *Ballistic Missile Defense* (New York: American Elsevier, 1971), p. 242.

83. Quoted by Yanarella, pp. 72–73.

84. Quoted by Leon Goure, *Civil Defense in the Soviet Union* (Berkeley: University of California Press, 1962), p. 14.

85. *Ibid.*, p. 33.

86. Quoted by Wolfe, *Soviet Strategy at the Crossroads*, p. 196.

87. C.L. Sulzberger, "Khrushchev Says in Interview He Is Ready to Meet Kennedy," *New York Times*, September 8, 1961, p. 10.

88. Saikowski and Gruliow, *Current Soviet Policies IV*, p. 158.

89. "Beseda tovarisha N.S. Khrushcheva," *Pravda*, July 18, 1962, p. 2.

90. Thomas W. Wolfe, *Soviet Power and Europe 1945–1970* (Baltimore: The Johns Hopkins Press, 1970), p. 187.

Robert P. Berman and John C. Baker, *Soviet Strategic Forces* (Washington, D.C.: Brookings Institution, 1982), p. 148.

91. Major General N.A. Talenskiy, "Anti-Missile Systems and Disarmament," *International Affairs* (October 1964): 17.

92. Trewitt, pp. 126–127.
93. Oral History Interview with Harold Brown, January 17, 1969, by Dorothy Pierce, Lyndon B. Johnson Library.
94. "Vazhnyye Problemy," *Pravda*, February 11, 1967, p. 3.
95. Henry A. Kissinger, *White House Years* (Boston: Little, Brown, 1979), p. 210.
96. Talbott, *Khrushchev Remembers: The Last Testament*, p. 533.

A Soviet defector reports that after Khrushchev, all strategic deception activities against the United States and its allies were centralized in a Chief Directorate for Strategic Deception of the Soviet General Staff, commanded by General Nikolai Ogarkov. Orgarkov, a Marshal of the Soviet Union, was until recently Chief of the General Staff. See *Inside the Soviet Army* by Viktor Suvorov (New York: Macmillan, 1982), p. 102.

97. Talbott, *Khrushchev Remembers*, p. 517.
98. *Department of Defense Appropriations for FY 1964*, p. 109.
99. *Ibid.*, p. 339.

Chapter 4. Alliance Politics and Nuclear Independence

1. Edward A. Kolodziej, *French International Policy Under de Gaulle and Pompidou* (Ithaca, NY: Cornell University Press, 1974), p. 47.
2. David Floyd, *Mao Against Khrushchev* (New York: Frederick A. Praeger, 1963), pp. 197–198.
3. Harry Schwartz, "Growing Internal Problems Strain Communist Unity," *New York Times*, November 11, 1962, p. E-3.
4. *Ibid.*
5. Raymond Aron, *Peace and War*, trans. Richard Howard and Annette Baker Fox (New York: Frederick A. Praeger, 1968), p. 536.
6. Quoted by Robert E. Osgood, *NATO—The Entangling Alliance* (Chicago: The University of Chicago Press, 1962), pp. 221–222.
7. *The Speeches, Remarks, Press Conferences, and Statements of Senator John F. Kennedy, August 1 Through November 7, 1960*, p. 981.
8. *Public Papers of the President of the United States—1961*, pp. 254–255.
9. Quoted by Dean Acheson, *A Review of North Atlantic Problems for the Future*, March 1961, LBJL, VPSF, Box 9, p. 32.

10. James L. Richardson, *Germany and the Atlantic Alliance* (Cambridge: Harvard University Press, 1966), p. 74.

11. National Security Council Policy Directive, *NATO and the Atlantic Nations*, April 20, 1961, LBJL, VPSF, Box 4, pp. 6–8.

12. *Facts on File* 21 (May 11–17, 1961): 175.

13. General Charles Ailleret, "Critique of Flexible Response," *Survival* 6 (November–December 1964): 259 and 262–263.

14. *Public Papers of the President of the United States – 1961*, p. 385.

15. *Facts on File* 21 (May 11–17, 1961): 174.

16. Schlesinger, pp. 329–330.

17. *Department of Defense Appropriations for FY 1963*, p. 8. Between 1961 and 1962, the Kennedy Administration raised the number of U.S. tactical nuclear weapons assigned to Western Europe by 60 percent, or by about 4,200 weapons. See Speech by Robert S. McNamara to the Economics Club of New York, November 18, 1963, DOD Press Release No. 1486-63, p. 16, Lyndon Baines Johnson Library, National Security File, Box 11. (Hereafter referred to as LBJL, NSF.)

18. Stewart Alsop, "Kennedy's Grand Strategy," p. 11.

19. Pierre Salinger, *With Kennedy* (New York: Doubleday, 1966), p. 227.

20. Quoted by Alastair Buchan and Philip Windsor, *Arms and Stability in Europe* (London: Chatto & Windus, 1963), p. 59.

21. David Halberstam, "The Programming of Robert Mc-Namara," *Harper's* 242 (February 1971): 37–71.

22. Text of McNamara Speech at University of Michigan, June 17, 1962.

23. *Public Papers of the President of the United States – 1962*, p. 402.

24. *Ibid.*, p. 513.

25. Chinese Government Statement on Test Ban Treaty, July 31, 1963, in *The Sino-Soviet Rift* by William E. Griffith (Cambridge: MIT Press, 1964), p. 327.

26. *Bulletin of the State Department* 19 (November 19, 1973): 653 and 655.

27. Richard E. Neustadt, *Alliance Politics* (New York: Cambridge University Press, 1970), pp. 32–33.

28. *Proposed US-UK Agreement for a Substitute Weapon Incident to Skybolt Cancellation*, December 17, 1962, p. 2, LBJL, VPSF, Box 9.

29. Richard E. Neustadt, *Report to the President: Skybolt and*

Nassau, November 15, 1963, p. 62, JFKL, NSF, Box 324.

30. *Ibid.*, p. 3.

31. *Public Papers of the President of the United States — 1962*, p. 909.

32. Neustadt quotes Ambassador Bohlen on p. 107 of his *Report to the President* that Bohlen blamed Undersecretary Ball for de Gaulle's rejection of the Nassau Agreement. His rationale was excised from the declassified version of Neustadt's report. The Ambassador made a similar charge in his memoirs. "... I am inclined to believe that something unexpected led de Gaulle to make his decision sooner than anticipated. That event possibly was the arrival of George Ball...." (Bohlen, p. 501.) One explanation for the ambassador's anger may be found in the reminiscences of Colonel LeRoy-Finville, the chief of Section 7, the clandestine operations branch of the *Service de Documentation Exterieure et de Contre-espionage*. In LeRoy-Finville's words:

> Instead of staying at the avenue Gabriel Embassy where he would be out of reach, Ball prefers staying at a hotel where he has complete freedom of movement. He does not want his comings and goings watched by his own associates. In this Paris which he loves, he has no intention of finding himself prisoner of the American diplomatic circle with its counsellors and Marines. We are aware of his habits and of his off-handedness. He is often away for hours, leaving in his room his briefcase stuffed with documents. What imprudence! The result is that, when he later meets his French opposite numbers, de Gaulle, Pompidou, Giscard, they already have in their pocket a summary of Ball's proposals and projects. This gives our negotiators a great advantage over the American. At the Hotel Majestic in Cannes, during the Kennedy round of 1964, we were to do even better: we drew materials from his notes every evening...

Quoted by Phillippe Bernert, *S.D.E.C.E. — Section 7* (Paris: Presses de la Cite, 1980), pp. 88–89.

George Ball argues that de Gaulle simply refused to take the MLF invitation seriously. See *The Past Has Another Pattern* by George W. Ball (New York: W.W. Norton, 1982), pp. 268–269.

33. Quoted by Neustadt, *Report to the President*, p. 110.

34. The Defense Department even considered leasing 100 ICBM silos in the continental U.S. to NATO if the alliance agreed to pay for construction and maintenance. The U.S., of course, would retain control of the missiles. McNamara conceded, however, that Bonn was unlikely to accept something blatantly American, costly, and unnecessary. See Memorandum of Conversation between Richard E.

Neustadt and Robert S. McNamara, November 21, 1964, LBJL, NSF, Box 12.

35. Richardson, pp. 69–70.

36. State Department Telegram, February 11, 1963, JFKL, NSF, Box 180.

37. "Major Powers Fear Spread of Nuclear Arms," *New York Times*, July 26, 1963.

38. O'Donnell and Powers, p. 349.

39. Quoted by Floyd, p. 249.

40. "China Defends Her Stand on Test Ban Treaty, August 15, 1963," in Griffith, p. 341.

41. Quoted by Alice Langley Hsieh, *Communist China's Strategy in the Nuclear Era* (Englewood Cliffs: Prentice-Hall, Inc., 1962), pp. 84 and 87.

42. Talbott, *Khrushchev Remembers — The Last Testament*, p. 258.

43. *Ibid.*, pp. 260–261.

44. "A Comment on the Soviet Government's Statement of August 21, 1963," in Griffith, p. 382.

45. Quoted by Floyd, p. 269.
Alfred Low, *The Sino-Soviet Dispute* (Rutherford, NJ: Fairleigh Dickinson University Press, 1976), p. 105.

46. Quoted by Floyd, pp. 273–274.

47. *Ibid.*, p. 275.

48. Sino-Soviet Task Force, Central Intelligence Agency, *The Sino-Soviet Dispute and Its Significance*, April 1, 1961, p. 9, JFKL, NSF, Box 176.

49. *Ibid.*, p. 11.

50. Parmet, *JFK: The Presidency of John F. Kennedy*, p. 83.

51. Notes on National Security Council Meeting, November 15, 1961, LBJL, VPSF, Box 4.

52. The first serious border clashes occurred in 1959.

53. Quoted in Central Intelligence Agency Memorandum, *Sino-Soviet Relations at a New Crisis*, January 14, 1963, p. 1, JFK, NSF, Box 180.

54. U.S. President, *Public Papers of the President of the United States* (Washington, D.C.: Government Printing Office, 1964), John F. Kennedy, January 1 to November 22, 1963, p. 18.

55. Glen T. Seaborg, *Kennedy, Khrushchev and the Test Ban* (Berkeley: University of California Press, 1981), p. 178.

56. *Ibid.*, p. 182.

57. *Ibid.*, pp. 186–187.

58. The Soviets were also trying to curry favor with the Chinese and this added to Moscow's reluctance to appear more desirous of a test ban treaty than the U.S. and Britain. Ambassador Anatoli Dobrynin let it be known on the Washington diplomatic circuit that the "time was not ripe for an agreement between the U.S. and the Soviet Union on any major issue." See Memorandum, Colonel Burris to Vice President Johnson, March 4, 1963, LBJL, VPSF, Box 6.

59. Speech contained in Mary Milling Lepper, *Foreign Policy Formulation—A Case Study of the Nuclear Test Ban Treaty of 1963* (Columbus, OH: Charles E. Merrill, 1971), p. 124.

60. Seaborg, p. 228.

President Kennedy probably asked this question privately. Summary notes of this meeting indicate that the Chinese issue was not raised. See Memorandum, Colonel Jackson to Vice President Johnson, July 9, 1963, LBJL, VPSF, Box 5.

61. Memorandum for Personal Files re President Kennedy & Red China, December 20, 1967, W. Averell Harriman Papers.

62. Schlesinger, p. 825.

On July 8, 1963, Walt Rostow, then Chairman of the Policy Planning Council at State, sent a memorandum to the president urging caution with the "Harriman Probe" to trade MLF for concessions from the Soviets during the test ban negotiations. "MLF," Rostow wrote, "probably constitutes a more powerful pressure on the Russians to think seriously about arms control than any other single element on the world scene, including the possibility of a Chinese Communist nuclear capability." JFKL, POF, Box 65.

A State Department Memorandum to Vice President Johnson, marked "Personal and Confidential," took a different tack. "Under any circumstances, the question [of] Communist China should be raised—primarily as a method of determining whether the non-aggression pact feelers are purely a political move which will be forgotten when they have served their purpose or whether they indicate something much more far-reaching in Soviet policy." See LBJL, VPSF, Box 5.

63. Tad Szulc, "Harriman Says Russians See Chinese A-Bomb Lag," *New York Times*, July 30, 1963, p. 1.

64. Quoted by Seaborg, p. 239.

65. Quoted by Floyd, p. 444.

66. Schlesinger, p. 829.

67. *Public Papers of the President of the United States—1963*, p. 602.

68. *Ibid.*, p. 623.

69. Memorandum, McGeorge Bundy to Bromley Smith, July 30, 1963; National Security Council Agenda, July 31, 1963; SNIE 13-4-63, July 31, 1963, JFKL, NSF, Box 314.

70. *Public Papers of the President of the United States — 1963*, p. 616.

71. *Ibid.*, p. 618.

72. "Statement of the Chinese Government Advocating the Complete, Thorough, Total, and Resolute Prohibition and Destruction of Nuclear Weapons, and Proposing a Conference of the Government Heads of All Countries of the World," in *The Chinese-Russian Dialogue I*, ed. Peter Beton (Los Angeles: University of Southern California School of International Affairs, 1964), p. 2.

73. Beton, "Soviet Government Statement, August 21, 1963," pp. 38 and 42.

74. Quoted by Alice Langley Hsieh, "The Sino-Soviet Nuclear Dialogue 1963," in *Sino-Soviet Military Relations 1945–66*, ed. Raymond L. Garthoff (New York: Frederick A. Praeger, 1966), p. 158.

75. Robert N. Estabrook, "Rusk Sides With Soviet in Red Rift," *Washington Post*, December 17, 1963, p. A-10.

The State Department claimed "substantial misinterpretation" in the Estabrook article. See Murray Marder, "Rusk's Comments on Soviet China Rift Explaining," *Washington Post*, December 18, 1963, p. A-10.

76. According to former CIA Director John McCone, the agency accurately forecast the Chinese explosion of a nuclear bomb. However, the CIA had no advance knowledge of Khrushchev's ouster. See Oral History Interview with John A. McCone by Joe B. Frantz, August 19, 1970, Lyndon Baines Johnson Library, pp. 19 and 21.

Chapter 5. Deterrence in Practice: Cuba 1962

1. U.S. Congress, Senate, *The Cuban Military Build-up: S. Rept.*, 88th Cong., 1st sess., 1963, pp. 5–6.

2. Cord Meyer, *Facing Reality* (New York: Harper and Row, 1980), pp. 227–228.

3. National Security Council Memorandum No. 181, JFKL, NSF, Box 338.

4. Robert F. Kennedy, *Thirteen Days* (New York: W.W. Norton, 1971), pp. 3–4.

5. Sorenson, p. 667.

6. Schlesinger, p. 749.

7. Quoted by David L. Larson, ed., *The 'Cuban Crisis' of 1962 — Selected Documents and Chronology* (Boston: Houghton Mifflin, 1963), pp. 10–11.

8. Thomas Powers, *The Man Who Kept the Secrets — Richard Helms and the CIA* (New York: Alfred A. Knopf, 1979), p. 101.

9. *Defense Appropriations for FY 1964*, p. 9.

10. Robert F. Kennedy, pp. 18–19.

11. Interview with Dean Rusk, Athens, Georgia, March 2, 1984.

12. *Public Papers of the President of the United States — 1962*, p. 806.

13. *Ibid.*, p. 808.

14. Foreign Broadcast Information Service, U.S.S.R. Daily Report, October 23, 1962, p. BB-22.

15. SIOP—1 July 1962, LBJL, NSF, Box 11.

16. Oral History Interview with Chester L. Cooper by Joseph E. O'Connor, May 6, 1966, p. 24.

17. Quoted by Robert F. Kennedy, pp. 67–68.

18. The connection between Khrushchev's letters of October 26 and 27 is still open to conjecture. However, a U.S. intelligence source reported at the time that the first letter to the president was written and dispatched personally by Khrushchev. Later, when Khrushchev discussed his reply with senior Soviet officials, violent objections were voiced, and the second letter containing the Turkish base proposal was dispatched. See World Highlights, November 11, 1962, LBJL, VPSF, Box 6.

19. Handwritten Note, Vice President Johnson, LBJL, VPSF, Box 8.

20. Secretary McNamara informed the president on April 25, 1963, that the last Jupiter launcher had been dismantled the day before and the last Jupiter warhead would be flown out of Turkey two days later. See Memo, Robert S. McNamara to John F. Kennedy, April 25, 1963, JFKL, POF, Box 117.

21. Claude Julien, "7 Hours with Mr. Castro," *Le Monde*, March 22, 1963, p. 6.

22. N.S. Khrushchev, *Prevent War, Safeguard Peace* (Moscow: Progress, 1963), p. 349.

23. *Ibid.*, pp. 353–354.

24. Talbott, *Khrushchev Remembers — The Last Testament*, p. 511.

25. A.A. Gromyko and B.N. Ponomarev, *Istoriya Vneshney Politiki SSSR* (Moscow: Nauka, 1981), p. 355.

26. James Reston, "What Was Killed Was Not Only the Presi-

dent But the Promise," *New York Times*, November 15, 1964, p. 126.

27. John G. Stoessinger, *Nations in Darkness* (New York: Random House, 1981), pp. 170–171.

28. Schlesinger, p. 750.

29. Ulam, p. 669.

Professor Ulam has since admitted that some of his colleagues have expressed reservations about his interpretation of the crisis. He maintains, however, that no alternative theory has been presented that explains "the apparently bizarre character of Soviet moves on Cuba." See Adam B. Ulam, *The Rivals* (New York: Viking, 1971), p. 325.

30. James Reston, "Khrushchev's Misjudgment on Cuba," *New York Times*, October 24, 1962.

The "trade" hypothesis is well argued by Michel Tatu in his book, *Power in the Kremlin* (New York: Viking, 1969), especially p. 241.

31. Arnold L. Horelick, *The Cuban Missile Crisis: Analysis of Soviet Calculations and Behavior* (Santa Monica, CA: Rand Corporation, 1963), pp. 12 and 57.

32. Carl A. Linden, *Khrushchev and the Soviet Leadership* (Baltimore: Johns Hopkins Press, 1966), p. 152.

33. *Public Papers of the President of the United States – 1962*, p. 898.

34. Julien, p. 6.

35. Talbott, *Khrushchev Remembers – The Last Testament*, p. 53.

36. Carsten Holbraad, *Superpowers and International Conflict* (New York: St. Martin's, 1979), p. 7.

37. Jacob D. Beam, *Unique Exposure* (New York: W.W. Norton, 1978), p. 293.

38. Memorandum, W. Walt Rostow to the Exec. Committee of the National Security Council, Nov. 10, 1962, LBJL, VPSF, Box 8.

39. Robert Alden, "Conventional, Not Atom, Arms Held NATO Need," *New York Times*, November 17, 1962.

40. *Defense Appropriations for FY 1964*, p. 31.

41. "The Lessons of the Cuban Missile Crisis," *Time* (September 27, 1982): 85.

42. "Learning from the Cuban Missile Crisis," *National Review* 34 (October 15, 1982): 1260.

43. Benjamin S. Lambeth, "Deterrence in the MIRV Era," *World Politics* 24 (January 1972): p. 232.

44. McGeorge Bundy, "The Presidency and the Peace," *Foreign Affairs* (April 1964): 359–360.

45. Khrushchev, *Prevent War, Safeguard Peace*, p. 352.

46. Quoted by Linden, p. 157.

Bibliography

Presidential Libraries

The Lyndon Baines Johnson Library, Austin, Texas (Vice Presidential Security Files, National Security Files, and White House Confidential Files).
The John F. Kennedy Memorial Library, Boston, Massachusetts (National Security Files and Presidential Office Files).

Archives

National Archives, Military History Division, Washington, D.C.
Personal Papers of the Honorable W. Averell Harriman, Washington, D.C.

Documents

Beton, Peter, ed. *The Chinese-Russian Dialogue.* 2 vols. Los Angeles: University of Southern California School of International Affairs, 1964–1965.
Foreign Broadcast Information Service, U.S.S.R. Daily Reports, 1960–1964.
Gruliow, Leo, ed. *Current Soviet Policies I: The Documentary Record of the 20th Communist Party Congress and Its Aftermath.* New York: Frederick A. Praeger, 1957.
_____, and Saikowski, Charlotte, eds. *Current Soviet Policies IV: The Documentary History of the 22nd Congress of the Communist Party of the Soviet Union.* New York: Frederick A. Praeger, 1962.
Larson, David L., ed. *The "Cuban Crisis" of 1962 – Selected*

Documents and Chronology. Boston: Houghton Mifflin Company, 1963.

Program of the Communist Party of the Soviet Union. Supplement to *New Times,* November 29, 1961.

New Frontiers of the Kennedy Administration: Texts of the Task Force Reports Prepared for the President. Washington, D.C.: Public Affairs Press, 1961.

U.S. Congress. House. Committee on Appropriations. *Department of Defense Appropriations for FY 1962: Hearings Before the Subcommittee on Defense Appropriations. Part III.* 87th Cong., 1st sess., 1961.

————. ————. ————. *Department of Defense Appropriations for FY 1963: Hearings Before The Subcommittee on Defense Appropriations. Part II.* 87th Cong., 2nd sess., 1962.

————. ————. ————. *Department of Defense Appropriations for FY 1964: Hearings Before the Subcommittee on Defense Appropriations. Part I.* 88th Cong., 1st sess., 1963.

————. ————. ————. *Department of Defense Appropriations for FY 1965: Hearings Before the Subcommittee on Defense Appropriations. Part I.* 88th Cong., 2nd sess., 1964.

U.S. Congress. Senate. *The Cuban Military Buildup. S. Rept.* 88th Cong., 1st sess., 1963.

————. ————. *Khrushchev's Speech of January 6, 1961 — A Summary and Interpretive Analysis. Senate Doc. 14.* 87th Cong., 1st sess., 1961.

————. ————. Committee on Armed Services. *Hearings on Military Aspects and Implications of Nuclear Test Ban Proposals and Related Matters.* 88th Cong., 1st sess. 1963.

————. ————. Committee on Commerce. *The Joint Appearances of Senator John F. Kennedy and Vice President Richard M. Nixon and Other 1960 Campaign Presentations. S. Rept. 994, Part III.* 87th Cong., 1st sess., 1961.

————. ————. ————. *The Speeches, Remarks, Press Conferences, and Statements of Senator John F. Kennedy, August 1 through November 7, 1960. S. Rept. 994, Part I.* 87th Cong., 1st sess., 1961.

U.S. Department of Defense. *Annual Report.* 1961–1965.

U.S. Federal Emergency Management Agency. *American Civil Defense 1945–1975.* Washington, D.C., 1980.

U.S. President. *Public Papers of the President of the United States.* Washington, D.C.: Government Printing Office, 1961–1963.

Whitney, Thomas P. *Khrushchev Speaks: Selected Speeches, Articles*

and Press Conferences, 1949–1961. Ann Arbor: University of
Michigan Press, 1963.

Newspapers and Magazines

The Atlantic
Facts on File
Harper's
Izvestia
Keesing's Contemporary Archives
Krasnaya Zvezda
Le Monde
The New Republic
Newsweek
New York Review of Books
The New York Times
Pravda
Saturday Evening Post
Time
U.S. News and World Report
Vital Speeches
Washington Post

Periodicals and Specialist Journals

Adelphi Papers
Air Force Magazine
Air University Quarterly Review
Army
Bulletin of the Atomic Scientists
Bulletin of the Department of State
Bulletin of the Institute for the Study of the U.S.S.R.
Current Digest of the Soviet Press
Current History
The Declassified Documents Quarterly Catalog
Foreign Affairs
Foreign Policy
Interavia
International Affairs (London)
International Affairs (Moscow)

International Security
Journal of Conflict Resolution
Kommunist
Kommunist Vooruzhennykh Sil
The Military Balance
Military Review
Morskoy Sbornik
New Times (Moscow)
Orbis
Political Science Quarterly
Problems of Communism
Public Policy
The Reporter
Royal United Services Institute Journal
Soviet Military Review
Strategic Review
Studies on the Soviet Union
Survey
Survival
The Wilson Quarterly
U.S. Naval Institute Proceedings
Voennyy Vestnik
Voenno-Istoricheskiy Zhurnal
World Politics

Unpublished Materials

Arnett, Robert L. "Soviet Attitudes Towards Nuclear War Survival (1962–1977): Has There Been a Change?" Ph.D. dissertation, Ohio State University, 1979.

Beachley, David R. "The Doctrine Gap: American Perceptions of Soviet Nuclear Doctrine and Strategy in the 1960s." Master's thesis, Georgetown University, 1982.

Collins, Edward M. "The Evolution of Soviet Strategy Under Khrushchev." Ph.D. dissertation, Georgetown University, 1966.

Monks, Alfred L. "Soviet Military Doctrine: 1964 to Armed Forces Day 1969." Ph.D. dissertation, University of Pennsylvania, 1968.

Spahr, William J. "The Soviet Military High Command 1957–1967: Political Socialization, Professionalization, and Modernization." Ph.D. dissertation, George Washington University, 1972.

Books

Adams, Benson D. *Ballistic Missile Defense*. New York: American Elsevier, 1971.

Aliano, Richard. *American Defense Policy from Eisenhower to Kennedy: The Politics of Changing Military Requirements*. Athens: Ohio University Press, 1975.

Allison, Graham T. *Essence of Decision*. Boston: Little, Brown, 1971.

Aspaturian, Vernon V. *Process and Power in Soviet Foreign Policy*. Boston: Little, Brown, 1971.

Bader, William B. *The United States and the Spread of Nuclear Weapons*. New York: Western, 1968.

Bagramyan, I. Kh. *Istoriya Voyn i Voennova Iskusstva*. Moscow: Voenizdat, 1970.

Bailey, Anthony. *Along the Edge of the Forest*. New York: Random House, 1983.

Ball, Desmond. *Politics and Force Levels: The Strategic Missile Program of the Kennedy Administration*. Berkeley: University of California, 1980.

Ball, George W. *The Past Has Another Pattern*. New York: W.W. Norton, 1982.

Bamford, James. *The Puzzle Palace: A Report on America's Most Secret Agency*. Boston: Houghton Mifflin, 1982.

Beam, Jacob D. *Unique Exposure*. New York: W.W. Norton, 1978.

Berman, Robert P., and Baker, John C. *Soviet Strategic Forces: Requirements and Responses*. Washington, D.C.: Brookings Institution, 1982.

Bernert, Phillippe. *S.D.E.C.E. — Section 7*. Paris: Presses de la Cite, 1980.

Bohlen, Charles E. *Witness to History 1929–1969*. New York: W.W. Norton, 1973.

Booth, Ken. *Strategy and Ethnocentrism*. New York: Holmes and Meier, 1979.

Bracken, Paul. *The Command and Control of Nuclear Forces*. New Haven, CT: Yale University Press, 1983.

Breslauer, George W. *Khrushchev and Brezhnev as Leaders: Building Authority in Soviet Politics*. London: George Allen and Unwin, 1982.

Brodie, Bernard, ed. *The Absolute Weapon*. New York: Harcourt, Brace, 1946.

_____. *Strategy in the Missile Age*. Princeton, NJ: Princeton University Press, 1959.

Brown, Neville. *Nuclear War: The Impending Strategic Deadlock*. London: Pall Mall, 1964.

Brown, Seymon. *The Forces of Power — Controversy and Change in United States Foreign Policy from Truman to Johnson*. New York: Columbia University Press, 1964.

Buckley, James L., and Warnke, Paul C. *Strategic Sufficiency: Fact or Fiction?* Washington, D.C.: American Enterprise Institute, 1972.

Burns, James MacGregor. *John Kennedy: A Political Profile*. New York: Harcourt, Brace, 1959.

Carrere d'Encausse, Helene. *Confiscated Power: How Soviet Russia Really Works*. New York: Harper and Row, 1982.

Chayes, Abram, and Wiesner, Jerome. *ABM: An Evaluation of the Decision to Deploy an Anti-Ballistic Missile System*. New York: Harper and Row, 1969.

Collins, John M. *U.S. — Soviet Military Balance, Concepts and Capabilities, 1960-1980*. New York: McGraw-Hill, 1980.

Crane, Robert D., ed. *Soviet Nuclear Strategy: A Critical Appraisal*. Washington, D.C.: Center for Strategic Studies, 1963.

_____, and Onacewicz, Wlodzimierz, eds. *Soviet Materials on Military Strategy: Inventory and Analysis for 1963*. Washington, D.C.: Center for Strategic Studies, 1964.

Crankshaw, Edward. *Khrushchev's Russia*. Great Britain: Penguin, 1962.

Dallin, David J. *Soviet Foreign Policy After Stalin*. New York: J.B. Lippincott, 1961.

Deane, Michael J. *Strategic Defense in Soviet Strategy*. Washington, D.C.: Advanced International Studies Institute, 1980.

Deutscher, Isaac. *Russia, China, and the West: A Contemporary Chronicle, 1953-1966*. London: Oxford University Press, 1970.

Dinerstein, Herbert S. *Fifty Years of Soviet Foreign Policy*. Baltimore: Johns Hopkins Press, 1968.

_____. *War and the Soviet Union: Nuclear Weapons and the Revolution in Soviet Military and Political Thinking*. Santa Monica, CA: Rand Corporation, 1959.

Divine, Robert A. *Eisenhower and the Cold War*. New York: Oxford University Press, 1981.

Dulles, Allen W. *The Craft of Intelligence*. New York: Harper and Row, 1963.

Dupuy, T.N. *Political-Military Affairs Since World War II: The Historical Setting for Current and Future Strategy*. Washington, D.C.: Historical Evaluation and Research Organization, 1965.

Edmonds, Robin. *Soviet Foreign Policy 1962-1973*. London: Oxford

University Press, 1975.

Erickson, John, ed. *The Military-Technical Revolution: Its Impact on Strategy and Foreign Policy.* New York: Frederick A. Praeger, 1966.

Fitzsimmons, Louise. *The Kennedy Doctrine.* New York: Random House, 1972.

Floyd, David. *Mao Against Khrushchev.* New York: Frederick A. Praeger, 1965.

Fuller, Helen. *Year of Trial: Kennedy's Crucial Decisions.* New York: Harcourt, Brace, 1962.

Gaddis, John Lewis. *Russia, the Soviet Union, and the United States: An Interpretive History.* New York: John Wiley, 1978.

Garthoff, Raymond L., ed. *Sino-Soviet Military Relations.* New York: Frederick A. Praeger, 1966.

_____. *The Soviet Image of Future War.* Washington, D.C.: Public Affairs, 1959.

_____. *Soviet Strategies in the Nuclear Age.* New York: Frederick A. Praeger, 1958.

Gavin, Lieutenant General James M. *War and Peace in the Space Age.* New York: Harper and Brothers, 1958.

Gehlen, Michael P. *The Politics of Coexistence.* Bloomington: Indiana University Press, 1967.

George, Alexander L., and Smoke, Richard. *Deterrence in American Foreign Policy: Theory and Practice.* New York: Columbia University Press, 1974.

Goure, Leon. *Civil Defense in the Soviet Union.* Berkeley: University of California Press, 1962.

Gray, Colin S. *Strategic Studies and Public Policy.* Lexington: University of Kentucky Press, 1982.

Griffith, William E. *The Sino-Soviet Split.* Cambridge: MIT Press, 1964.

Gromyko, A.A., and Ponomarev, B.N. *Istoriya Vneshney Politiki SSSR 1945–1980.* Moscow: Nauka, 1981.

Halberstam, David. *The Best and the Brightest.* New York: Random House, 1972.

Hanak, H. *Soviet Foreign Policy Since the Death of Stalin.* London: Routledge and Kegan Paul Ltd., 1972.

Harriman, W. Averell. *America and Russia in a Changing World.* Garden City, NY: Doubleday, 1971.

Hilsman, Roger. *To Move a Nation.* New York: Dell, 1967.

Holbraad, Carsten. *Superpowers and International Conflict.* New York: St. Martin's, 1979.

Holloway, David. *The Soviet Union and the Arms Race*. New Haven, CT: Yale University Press, 1983.

Holst, Johan J. *Comparative U.S. and Soviet Deployments, Doctrines, and Arms Limitations*. Chicago: University of Chicago Press, 1971.

Horelick, Arnold L., and Rush, Myron. *Strategic Power and Soviet Foreign Policy*. Santa Monica, CA: Rand Corporation, 1965.

Hsieh, Alice Langley. *Communist China and Nuclear Force*. Santa Monica, CA: Rand Corporation, 1963.

————. *Communist China's Strategy in the Nuclear Era*. Englewood Cliffs, NJ: Prentice-Hall, Inc., 1962.

Kahan, Jerome H. *Security in the Nuclear Age*. Washington, D.C.: Brookings Institution, 1975.

Kahn, Herman. *On Thermonuclear War*. Princeton, NJ: Princeton University Press, 1960.

Kaufmann, William W. *The McNamara Strategy*. New York: Harper and Row, 1964.

Kennan, George F. *Memoirs 1925–1950*. Boston: Little, Brown, 1967.

Kennedy, John F. *The Strategy of Peace*. New York: Harper and Brothers, 1960.

————. *Why England Slept*. 2nd ed. New York: Wilfred Funk, 1961.

Kennedy, Robert F. *Thirteen Days*. New York: W.W. Norton, 1971.

Khrushchev, N.S. *Communism—Peace and Happiness for the Peoples*. 2 vols. Moscow: Foreign Language Publishing House, 1963.

————. *Imperialism—Enemy of the People, Enemy of Peace. Selected Passages, 1956–1963*. Moscow: Foreign Language Publishing House, 1963.

————. *Prevent War, Safeguard Peace*. Moscow: Progress Publishers, 1963.

Kinnard, Douglas. *The Secretary of Defense*. Lexington: University of Kentucky Press, 1980.

Kintner, William R., ed. *Safeguard: Why the ABM Makes Sense*. New York: Hawthorne Books, 1969.

Kir'yana, Lieutenant General M.M. *Voenno-Tekhnicheskiy Progress i Vooryzhennyye Sily SSSR*. Moscow: Voenizdat, 1982.

Kissinger, Henry A. *Nuclear Weapons and Foreign Policy*. New York: Harper and Row, 1957.

————. *White House Years*. Boston: Little, Brown, 1979.

Klass, Philip J. *Secret Sentries in Space*. New York: Random House, 1971.

Kolkowicz, Roman. *The Soviet Army and the Communist Party: Institutions in Conflict.* Santa Monica, CA: Rand Corporation, 1966.

Knorr, Klaus, and Read, Thornton, eds. *Limited Strategic War, Essays on Nuclear Strategy.* New York: Frederick A. Praeger, 1962.

Kohl, Wilfrid L. *French Nuclear Diplomacy.* Princeton, NJ: Princeton University Press, 1971.

Kohler, Foy D. *Understanding the Russians.* New York: Harper and Row, 1970.

Kolodziej, Edward A. *French International Policy Under de Gaulle and Pompidou.* Ithaca, NY: Cornell University Press, 1974.

Kozlov, General S.N. *O Sovetskoy Voennoy Nauke.* Moscow: Voenizdat, 1964. Translated by the U.S. Air Force Foreign Technology Division, FTD-HT-66-259, 1966.

Kulski, W.W. *Peaceful Coexistence—An Analysis of Soviet Foreign Policy.* Chicago: Henry Regnery, 1959.

Leebaert, Derek, ed. *Soviet Military Thinking.* London: George Allen and Unwin, 1980.

Legault, Albert. *Deterrence and the Atlantic Alliance.* Toronto: Canadian Institute of International Affairs, 1966.

Linden, Carl A. *Khrushchev and the Soviet Leadership 1957–1964.* Baltimore: Johns Hopkins Press, 1966.

Lippmann, Walter. *The Coming Tests with Russia.* Boston: Little, Brown, 1961.

Lockwood, Jonathan Samuel. *The Soviet View of U.S. Strategic Doctrine.* New Brunswick, NJ: Transaction, 1983.

Lomov, Colonel-General N.A. *Sovetskaya Voennaya Doktrina.* Moscow: Znaniye, 1963. Translated by the Joint Publications Research Service, No. 21678, October 31, 1963.

Low, Alfred D. *The Sino-Soviet Dispute.* Rutherford, NJ: Fairleigh Dickinson University Press, 1976.

Lowe, George E. *The Age of Deterrence.* Boston: Little, Brown, 1964.

Mackintosh, J.M. *Strategy and Tactics of Soviet Foreign Policy.* London: Oxford University Press, 1962.

McNamara, Robert S. *The Essence of Security: Reflections in Office.* New York: Harper and Row, 1968.

McSherry, James E. *Khrushchev and Kennedy in Retrospect.* Palo Alto, CA: Open Door, 1971.

Malinovskiy, Marshal R. Ya. *Bditel'no Stoyat Na Strazhe Mira.* Moscow: Voenizdat, 1963.

Mandelbaum, Michael. *The Nuclear Question: The United States and*

Nuclear Weapons, 1946–1976. New York: Cambridge University Press, 1979.

Martin, Lawrence, ed. *Strategic Thought in the Nuclear Age*. Baltimore: Johns Hopkins University Press, 1979.

Medvedev, Roy. *Khrushchev*. Garden City, NY: Anchor/Doubleday, 1983.

_____, and Medvedev, Zhores. *Khrushchev: The Years in Power*. New York: W.W. Norton, 1978.

Meyer, Cord. *Facing Reality*. New York: Harper and Row, 1980.

Miller, Mark E. *Soviet Strategic Power and Doctrine: The Quest for Superiority*. Washington, D.C.: Advanced International Studies Institute, 1982.

Miroff, Bruce. *Pragmatic Illusions, the Presidential Politics of John F. Kennedy*. New York: David McKay, 1976.

Neustadt, Richard E. *Alliance Politics*. New York: Cambridge University Press, 1970.

Nixon, Richard M. *Leaders*. New York: Warner, 1982.

O'Donnell, Kenneth P., and Powers, David F. *Johnny, We Hardly Knew Ye*. Boston: Little, Brown, 1970.

Osgood, Robert E. *Limited War*. Chicago: University of Chicago Press, 1957.

_____. *NATO—The Entangling Alliance*. Chicago: University of Chicago Press, 1962.

Paper, Lewis J. *The Promise and the Performance: The Leadership of John F. Kennedy*. New York: Crown, 1975.

Parment, Herbert S. *J.F.K.—The Presidency of John F. Kennedy*. New York: Dial, 1983.

_____. *Jack: The Strategy of John F. Kennedy*. New York: Dial, 1980.

Peeters, Paul. *Massive Retaliation: The Policy and Its Critics*. Chicago: Henry Regnery, 1959.

Penkovskiy, Oleg. *The Penkovskiy Papers*. Garden City, NY: Doubleday, 1965.

Powers, Gary Francis. *Operation Overflight*. New York: Holt Rinehart and Winston, 1970.

Powers, Thomas. *The Man Who Kept the Secrets—Richard Helms and the C.I.A.* New York: Alfred A. Knopf. 1979.

Prados, John. *The Soviet Estimate*. New York: Dial, 1982.

Pringle, Peter, and Arkin, William. *S.I.O.P.—The Secret U.S. Plan for Nuclear War*. New York: W.W. Norton, 1983.

Quester, George H. *Nuclear Diplomacy: The First Twenty-Five Years*. New York: Dunellen, 1970.

Rapaport, Anatol. *The Big Two — Soviet-American Perceptions of Foreign Policy*. New York: Pegasus, 1971.

Richardson, James L. *Germany and the Atlantic Alliance*. Cambridge: Harvard University Press, 1966.

Roherty, James M. *Decisions of Robert S. McNamara*. Coral Gables, FL: University of Miami Press, 1980.

Rositzke, Harry. *The KGB: The Eyes of Russia*. Garden City, NY: Doubleday, 1981.

Rostow, W.W. *View from the Seventh Floor*. New York: Harper and Row, 1964.

Salinger, Pierre. *With Kennedy*. Garden City, NY: Doubleday, 1966.

Savinkin, N.I., and Bogolyubov, K.M. *KPSS o Vooruzhennykh Silakh Sovetskovo Soyuza*. Moscow: Voenizdat, 1981.

Schelling, Thomas C. *Arms and Influence*. New Haven, CT: Yale University Press, 1966.

Schlesinger, Arthur M., Jr. *A Thousand Days*. Boston: Houghton Mifflin, 1965.

Schwartz, Harry, ed. *Russia Enters the 1960's*. New York: J.B. Lippincott, 1962.

Scott, Harriet F. *Soviet Military Doctrine: Its Continuity 1960–1970*. Menlo Park, CA: Stanford Research Institute, 1971.

_____. *Soviet Military Doctrine: Its Formulation and Dissemination*. Menlo Park, CA: Stanford Research Institute, 1971.

_____, and Scott, William F. *The Armed Forces of the USSR*. Boulder, CO: Westview Press, 1978.

Scott, William F. *Sources of Military Doctrine and Strategy*. New York: Crane, Rusak, 1975.

Seaborg, Glenn F. *Kennedy, Khrushchev and the Test Ban*. Berkeley: University of California Press, 1981.

Sejna, Jan. *We Will Bury You*. London: Sidgewick and Jackson, 1982.

Sidey, Hugh. *John F. Kennedy, President*. New York: Atheneum, 1964.

Sobel, Lester A., ed. *Russia's Rulers: The Khrushchev Period*. New York: Facts on File, 1971.

Sokolovskiy, Marshal V.D. *Soviet Military Strategy*. Translated and with an Analytic Introduction by Herbert S. Dinerstein, Leon Goure and Thomas W. Wolfe. Englewood Cliffs, NJ: Prentice-Hall, 1963.

_____. *Soviet Military Strategy*. 3rd ed. Translated by Harriet F. Scott. New York: Crane, Rusak, 1975.

_____. *Voennaya Strategia*. With an Analytic Introduction by Raymond L. Garthoff. London: Pall Mall Press, 1963.

Sorenson, Theodore C. *Kennedy*. New York: Harper and Row, 1965.

Stoessinger, John G. *Nations in Darkness — China, Russia, and America*. New York: Random House, 1981.

Talbott, Strobe, ed. *Khrushchev Remembers*. Boston: Little, Brown, 1970.

_____. *Khrushchev Remembers — The Last Testament*. Boston: Little, Brown, 1974.

Tang, Peter S.H. *The Twenty-Second Congress of the Communist Party of the Soviet Union and Moscow-Tirana-Peking Relations*. Washington, D.C.: Research Institute on the Sino-Soviet Bloc, 1962.

Tatu, Michel. *Power in the Kremlin*. New York: Viking, 1969.

Tolubko, V.F. *Nedelin*. Moscow: Molodaya Gvardiya, 1979.

Trewhitt, Henry L. *McNamara: His Ordeal in the Pentagon*. New York: Harper and Row, 1971.

Tully, Andrew. *The Super Spies*. New York: William Morrow, 1969.

Ulam, Adam B. *Dangerous Relations: The Soviet Union in World Politics, 1970–1982*. New York: Oxford University Press, 1983.

_____. *Expansion and Coexistence: The History of Soviet Foreign Policy 1917–1967*. New York: Praeger, 1968.

_____. *The Rivals: America and Russia since World War II*. New York: Viking, 1971.

Vigor, Peter H. *The Soviet View of War, Peace and Neutrality*. London: Routledge and Kegan Paul, 1975.

Walton, Richard J. *Cold War and Counterrevolution, the Foreign Policy of John F. Kennedy*. New York: Viking, 1972.

Watt, D.C. *Survey of International Affairs 1961*. London: Oxford University Press, 1965.

Whiting, Kenneth R. *Soviet Reactions to American Military Strategy*. Maxwell Air Force Base, AL: Air University Press, 1965.

Wise, David, and Ross, Thomas B. *The U-2 Affair*. New York: Random House, 1962.

Weeks, Albert L. *The Other Side of Coexistence: An Analysis of Russian Foreign Policy*. New York: Pitman, 1970.

Werth, Alexander. *Russia Under Khrushchev*. Greenwich: Crest, 1962.

West, Nigel. *The Circus: MI-5 Operations 1945–72*. Briarcliff Manor, NY: Stein and Day, 1983.

Wolfe, Thomas W. *The Global Strategic Perspective from Moscow*. Santa Monica, CA: Rand Corporation, 1973.

_____. *A Postscript on the Significance of the Book Soviet Military Strategy*. Santa Monica, CA: Rand Corporation, 1965.

_____. *Soviet Power and Europe — 1945-1970*. Baltimore: Johns Hopkins University Press, 1970.

_____. *Soviet Strategy at the Crossroads*. Cambridge: Harvard University Press, 1964.

_____. *The Soviet Voice in the East-West Strategic Dialogue*. Santa Monica, CA: Rand Corporation, 1964.

Yanarella, Ernest J. *The Missile Defense Controversy*. Lexington: University Press of Kentucky, 1977.

York, Herbert. *Race to Oblivion: A Participant's View of the Arms Race*. New York: Simon and Schuster, 1970.

Zagoria, Donald S. *The Sino-Soviet Conflict 1956-1961*. New York: Atheneum, 1964.

Zimmerman, William. *Soviet Perspectives on International Relations*. Princeton, NJ: Princeton University Press, 1969.

Zuckerman, Solly. *Scientists and War*. New York: Harper and Row, 1967.

Index